Database Management Systems

A Technical Review

Alan Mayne

PUBLISHED BY NCC PUBLICATIONS

British Library Cataloguing in Publication Data

Mayne, Alan
    Database management systems.
    1. Data base management
    I. Title
    001.64'42   QA76.9.D3
    ISBN 0-85012-323-2

First published in 1981 by:

NCC Publications, The National Computing Centre Limited, Oxford Road, Manchester M1 7ED, England.

Typeset in 10pt. Times Roman and printed by
UPS Blackburn Limited, 76-80 Northgate, Blackburn, Lancashire.

ISBN 0-85012-323-2

Acknowledgments

The author wishes to thank the following people who have commented on the material used to compile this book:

R L Jenkinson	Adabas Software Ltd
C Hutchinson	Adabas Software Ltd
W R Pilgrim	Sperry Univac
R Holloway	ICL
A Milner	Cullinane UK (formerly ICL)
F Kornhauser	IBM
M B Jones	IBM
J Cushley	Cincom Systems
D Gillett	Cincom Systems
M Newton	Open University
I Douglas	NCC
R Morton	NCC

Thanks are also due to the following organisations for providing the information used to compile the book:

Adabas Software Limited, Derby
Sperry Univac, London
Scicon Limited, London
Cullinane Corporation (UK) Limited, London
ICL Limited, London
IBM United Kingdom Limited, London
Cincom Systems Limited, Maidenhead

The Centre acknowledges with thanks the support provided by the Computers, Systems and Electronics Requirements Board (CSERB) and the Commission of the European Communities for the project from which this publication derives.

Preface

This book is a technical review of some of the major Database Management Systems (DBMS). It assumes that the reader has a good general knowledge of data processing and has read some introductory material about database.

The objective of the book is to describe the major facilities provided by a number of DBMSs and explain how these work. This is done by comparing, on a facility-by-facility basis, the following DBMSs:

— ADABAS;

— DMS 1100;

— IDMS (Cullinane and ICL products);

— IMS-DL/1;

— TOTAL.

Since these systems are continually being enhanced, the book concentrates on the major features and principles which are unlikely to change dramatically.

The book will be useful to:

— organisations which are in the process of selecting a DBMS;

— training organisations running database courses;

— existing users of one of the systems described as a training aid;

— computing science students interested in database and DBMS implementation techniques.

Contents

1 Introduction

SCOPE AND BACKGROUND

It is first necessary to explain what is meant by a DBMS. Before this can be done it is necessary to define *database:*

> 'A database is a collection of stored data organised in such a way that all user data requirements are satisfied by the database. In general there is only one copy of each item of data although there may be controlled repetition of some data.' (See item 6 in bibliography.)

Given this definition it is now possible to state the formal definition of a DBMS:

> 'A database management system is a general-purpose set of programs that aid and control each user's access to and use of the database for adding, modifying and retrieving data, and this includes facilities giving data independence, integrity and security.' (See item 6 in bibliography.)

It is assumed that the reader is already familiar with the general concepts of 'database'. Consequently this book does not include a description of what a database is, nor does it discuss the claimed benefits and disadvantages of database. The objective is to describe the major facilities provided by a number of DBMSs and to explain, in general terms, how these facilities work.

In order to achieve this objective, five widely used DBMSs, which are representative of the types of DBMS software available, are compared on a facility-by-facility basis. This approach highlights the differences between the various DBMSs and illustrates the different ways in which a given facility may be implemented. The five DBMSs described and the organisations responsible for them are:

ADABAS	Adabas Software Limited
DMS 1100	Sperry Univac
IDMS	The Cullinane Corporation and International Computers Limited (ICL)
IMS-DL/1	International Business Machines Limited (IBM)
TOTAL	Cincom Systems Limited

Both DMS 1100 and IDMS are known as 'CODASYL' systems, ie their basic philosophy and the facilities which they provide are based on the recommendations endorsed by CODASYL, the Conference of Data Systems Languages. CODASYL is generally responsible for the development of the COBOL programming language. However, the database facilities are also applicable to other programming languages. Although both of these DBMSs are based on the same recommendations, there are differences in the facilities actually supported and in the way they are implemented. The inclusion of descriptions of two similar systems has resulted in limited duplication of some information. In many cases the differences between the two systems are subtle.

The descriptions of the DBMSs were compiled by studying the vendors' literature. This included basic sales brochures, programmer reference manuals and documentation containing information about the internal organisation of the systems. With the exception of IBM, all the vendors were visited in order to clarify various points and obtain further information. A draft description of each system was then produced and its vendor was invited to comment. All the vendors provided constructive comments which allowed a number of errors to be corrected and various other improvements to be made to the text. However, if any errors remain they are the author's responsibility.

The vendors of DBMSs are continually improving their products. Consequently, a book providing very detailed descriptions would rapidly become out-of-date. This book does not attempt to provide definitive descriptions. Instead, it aims to describe, in general terms, how the systems operate. Some DBMS facilities are not covered; for example, special recovery facilities which are not widely used. For this reason, organisations using this book to help them select a DBMS are urged to contact the vendors in order to ensure that they base their decision on up-to-date information. That the book does not say that a given feature is supported by a DBMS does not necessarily imply that the feature does not exist or that there are no other ways of fulfilling the requirement. As the book concentrates on the major features, which are unlikely to change dramatically, it should be a useful reference for a considerable period of time.

THE STRUCTURE OF THE BOOK

This book is divided into the following chapters:

1   Introduction
2   Logical Structuring and Data Independence
3   Security and Integrity
4   Language Interfaces
5   Internals
6   Installation and Operation

Chapters 2, 3 and 4 each cover one of what the author considers to be the three most important aspects of a DBMS. The detailed structure of this book, as presented in the contents list, may be used as a frame of reference for comparing any DBMS. Alternatively, a detailed list and discussion of selection criteria may be found in items 2 and 3 (see bibliography).

The logical structuring facilities are important because these influence the way in which application systems are designed and implemented. They determine how the natural relationships between an organisation's data may be modelled for implementation on the computer. Chapter 2 also includes a discussion of Data Independence.

The security and integrity facilities described in Chapter 3 are clearly vital. In the event of the database being damaged in any way it is essential that it can be repaired. As the data in the database is shared between a number of users, it may be desirable or even necessary to specify access control constraints in order to prevent unauthorised access. Sharing of data may also cause problems if the database may be updated. The DBMS must be able to protect the integrity of the data in the event, for example, of two different programs attempting to update the same data concurrently.

The interface between the users of a DBMS and the system itself is clearly important. Here, a user means anybody who interfaces directly with the DBMS itself. This includes application programmers and the people responsible for describing the required database to the system. The language interfaces with the DBMS determine the power of the system for manipulating data. Their ease of use, or otherwise, will strongly influence the training overheads and will be reflected in the error rate or debugging time during programming.

Chapter 5 reviews the more technical aspects of the DBMSs. It describes how the various DBMSs interface with the computer's operating system. There is also a detailed description of how the data is stored in physical storage and how the logical data structures are implemented. This information will be of particular interest to database systems (software) programmers. A knowledge of the internals of a DBMS is also invaluable to the people who design the (physical) database in order to produce an efficient system.

The final chapter considers the installation of the DBMS and its maintenance when in use. It describes the facilities provided for restructuring and reorganising the database as it grows and changes. The performance of an operational system can also cause major headaches so facilities for monitoring and tuning are discussed. The specific problems of optimising storage requirements and access times are also important so the facilities provided (with the DBMS) to assist in this area are presented.

HOW TO USE THIS BOOK

This book is organised so that it may be used in a variety of ways:

— *Serially:* The book may be read in its entirety from start to finish. When used in this way the reader will notice some repetition of information, especially in Chapter 2 and generally in the entries for DMS 1100 and IDMS. Chapter 4 may prove to be 'heavy' reading but it may safely be 'browsed' through as subsequent chapters are not dependent upon it. Readers who are not interested in the technical detail may bypass Chapter 5 although small parts of Chapter 6 are dependent upon it.

— *Sequentially for a Management Overview:* A busy manager who is not concerned with the technical discussion may bypass the entries about the five DBMSs.

— *Sequentially by DBMS:* A reader who is primarily interested in one particular DBMS can bypass the entries for the others. Within any given section, each entry is independent of the others; information has been repeated where necessary to allow the book to be used in this way.

— *Indexed:* The contents list at the front of the book, or the index at the back enables the book to be used as a general reference book.

— *Direct:* Information may be accessed directly if the page number is known.

TERMINOLOGY

In a book of this kind, terminology poses special problems. Each DBMS has its own set of jargon. A standard set of terms for use throughout the book was considered but it was thought that this would make it more difficult for the reader to transfer to the vendors' documentation, especially if the book is used as part of a training course. Therefore, the vendors' terminology has been used. It is hoped that the reader can slip from one to another without confusion. The only exception to this is that the term 'field' has been used throughout since it is easier to write, type and speak than 'data-item' or 'data-element'.

2 Logical Structuring and Data Independence

The objectives of this chapter are to:

— explain the importance of logical structuring and data independence facilities;

and for each of the five DBMSs to:

— describe the overall architecture of the system;

— explain how data can be arranged as fields, groups, records and files;

— describe how different record types may be related together in order to model the natural relationships between them;

— consider what level of data independence is supported.

INTRODUCTION

The definition of a database in Chapter 1 states that it is a collection of stored data organised in such a way that all user data requirements are satisfied by it. The individual items of data held by a database do not exist in isolation to each other; they are related in some way. For example, the items representing a person's name, height, weight and age are related and may be conveniently 'grouped' together.

The relationships between the data can be more complex. If a person owns a number of motor cars there is a one-to-many relationship between that person and the details of the cars owned. If a number of people jointly own a fleet of cars there is a many-to-many relationship between the people details and the car details. Each person is the part-owner of a number of cars and each car is owned by a number of people.

The identification of the fundamental groups of data and their relationships, in a way which is independent of any computer implementation, is called *data modelling*. Data modelling is the first stage in designing a database. If it is not done properly before the database is implemented some of the benefits of adopting the database approach will be lost. Data modelling and database design are beyond the scope of this book (see items 7 and 9 in the Bibliography).

A DBMS must therefore provide facilities which allow these natural relationships between items of data to be represented. In other words, the DBMS should be capable of modelling the logical structure of the data in some way. The ease, or otherwise, with which the data model can be implemented, using the logical structuring facilities provided, can have a significant effect on the effort required to design the database and develop application systems. If the structuring facilities of a DBMS are limited, excessive duplication of data may occur and special 'tricks' may be necessary to program around its shortcomings. When an organisation is choosing a DBMS, it should ensure that the structuring facilities are capable of modelling its data in a clear and natural way.

At this point in the discussion it is useful to explain what is meant by the terms *record* and *record type*. *Record type* is used as a collective term for all records which describe similar objects. The term *record* is used when a single record, which describes one occurrence of the object, is being discussed.

Relationships between items of data are implemented by allowing them to be combined into groups and records. These are termed *inter-field* or sometimes *intra-record* relationships. The more complex one-to-many relationships are represented by either allowing a group to be repeated within a record or by relating record types together in some way. Relationships between different records are called *inter-record* relationships. The types of relationships supported by the five DBMSs are described later in this chapter.

The definition of a DBMS in Chapter 1 says that it should 'include facilities for giving data independence'. Data independence allows the physical or logical structure of the data to be altered without changing the data as seen by the application programs. This facility is responsible for producing some of the benefits which can result from using database software. Consequently, the level of data independence offered by a

DBMS is very important and should be seriously investigated if a system is being selected.

In order to illustrate some of the benefits that derive from data independence it is useful to consider how programs are dependent on the data when conventional files are used. Each program using a file contains the definition of a format of the record type (or possibly types) held on the file. The program logic also assumes the structure of the file; for example, its processing sequence. This is especially true if the file contains multiple record types such as batch header, batch detail and batch total record types.

If the format or structure of the file is changed in any way, all the programs using it must be modified. For example, if a new field is added to a file to support a new program, every existing program which uses the file will require maintenance even though not actually using the new field. In this simple example the existing programs only need to be recompiled. However, there could be hundreds of existing programs. This illustrates how a superficially simple change can prove to be a long and costly operation.

Another form of maintenance which is sometimes required is altering the length of a field. Clearly, programs making use of the field will be directly affected and their logic will need to be checked. At first sight it may be thought that programs which do not actually use the field only need to be recompiled. Alas, this may not be true. If the record, or the group field containing the field whose length is to be altered, is moved to a working storage area by the program, the record description of the working storage area will also need to be changed. For example, if a record is transferred to a work file by the program, the record description for the work file must also be changed. Consequently, the logic of all the programs which use the file must be checked, including those which do not actually use the field concerned.

The examples cited above demonstrate some of the maintenance problems associated with conventional files. These problems can be overcome by making application programs independent of the way this is organised. Three types of independence can be identified.

— *Device Independence.* Programs are independent of the physical devices on which the data is stored. All the DBMSs provide this level of independence. In fact, the data management facilities of good operating systems provide it for conventional files.

— *Physical Data Independence*. Programs are independent of the way in which the data is physically organised. This implies that it should be possible to change the physical positions of the records in the database. It should also be possible to change the physical format of the data, eg from binary to floating point. Changes to the record structure or inter-record relationships are considered to be logical changes.

— *Logical Data Independence*. This allows the logical structure to be changed without affecting the application program's view of the data. This suggests that it should be possible to change the structure of a record type. For example, new fields could be added, existing fields reordered or their sizes changed, and unused fields deleted. It also implies that relationships could be added, changed or deleted.

Complete data independence is very costly to provide both in terms of software and hardware resources. As a result no known DBMS offers full data independence. The DBMS developers have had to compromise between the ideal of full independence and the implementational difficulties in providing it.

In order to discuss the logical structuring and data independence facilities supported by the five DBMSs it is necessary to introduce some basic concepts and terminology. Therefore, the next two sections describe the overall architecture of the systems and the data groupings supported respectively.

In order to provide data independence the DBMS has to map the data between its physical representation and the program's logical view. The process of marrying together the program's view with the data in physical storage is known as *binding*.

OVERALL ARCHITECTURE

This section briefly describes the overall architecture of the five DBMSs. The aim is to introduce some of the basic terminology associated with the systems.

ADABAS

ADABAS is based on partially-inverted file structures. The ADABAS Data Dictionary holds the 'conceptual', physical and logical views of the data. The conceptual view comprises standard field and file definitions for organisation functions. The physical view is the definition of the ADABAS database files and fields which are held in the ADABAS system file called the ASSOCIATOR. Logical views or 'userviews' are individual application views of data in the application specified format and order regardless of how it is stored on the ADABAS database.

DMS 1100

DMS 1100 is based on the CODASYL proposals. It has two levels of data definition. The highest level is the SCHEMA which defines all the data, relationships and device media control parameters for the database. It is described using a Data Description Language. The SCHEMA information is stored in a database (termed a 'meta database'), and is also translated into a module which is used at run time.

The second level of data definition is the SUBSCHEMA which defines a subset of the SCHEMA view of the database. It allows a local view of the database to be defined which describes the components that may be accessed, and how they may be used, by an application system.

The SUBSCHEMA is defined by a Subschema Data Definition Language (SDDL). A SCHEMA will usually have a number of SUBSCHEMAs associated with it. Each SUBSCHEMA will describe a different application view of the database. This information is also stored in the 'meta database' and in subschema modules which are used at run time.

IDMS

IDMS is also based on the CODASYL proposals. It has three levels of data definition. The highest level, the SCHEMA, specifies all the data descriptions, data relationships and input/output parameters for the database. It is specified by using a 'Schema Data Description Language'. The SCHEMA information is stored in a special IDMS file called the DIRECTORY.

The second level, the Device Media Control Block (DMCB), provides the mapping information between the logical and physical descriptions of the data. The DMCB is specified by using a Device Media Control or Service Description Language. There can be one or more Device Media Control Blocks describing either the whole or a subset of the database.

This information is stored in the DIRECTORY and in control block modules which are loaded and used when database applications are executed.

The final level, the SUBSCHEMA, describes a subset of the database which allows a local view of the database to be defined for an application. It defines which components in the database may be accessed and how they may be accessed.

A 'Subschema Data Description Language' is used to describe the SUBSCHEMA. There are usually a number of SUBSCHEMAs describing different 'views' of the data and providing various access authorities. This information is also stored in the DIRECTORY and in Subschema modules which are loaded and used at run time.

IMS-DL/1

The data on a DL/1 database is described by one or more Data Base Definition (DBD) modules. Each DBD describes one PHYSICAL DATABASE. A PHYSICAL DATABASE defines one physical record type.

A logical record is defined in terms of one or more SEGMENTS. A SEGMENT is equivalent to a repeating group in a conventional record.

The DBD module is generated by a utility. Input to the utility describes the physical data set (ie file) and the structure of the record. Information needed to relate segments in one record type to those in other record types is also specified. DL/1 loads the DBD module at execution time and uses it to access the data.

The DBD, which describes a Physical Database, may be thought of as a definition of a physical file and record type it contains. A DL/1 database contains at least one, usually many, physical files. The global view of the DL/1 database is implicitly described by all the various DBD modules which define the physical files that comprise the database.

A Data Base Definition is also used to relate segments within different record types, and therefore different Physical Databases. Such a DBD is called a Logical Database.

The programmer's local view of the database is defined in a Program Specification Block (PSB). The PSB contains one or more Program Communication Blocks (PCBs). A PCB is defined for each Data Base

Definition that the program may access. Each PCB defines which segments within the physical or logical database the programmer may access and the type of access allowed. DL/1 is not a CODASYL system but the PSB may be compared with a subschema.

TOTAL

The data on a TOTAL database is represented by one or more Data Base Definition Modules, known as DBMODs. TOTAL's Data Base Definition Language (DBDL) is used to generate the DBMODs. The DBMOD is loaded from the program library by TOTAL at run time, and used to access the database.

A global view of the database could be produced by generating a DBMOD which describes the whole database. Normally, however, a number of different local views, which may have some degree of commonality, will be generated for different application systems. Each local view will define the subset of the database needed for a particular application or a series of applications. The global view of the database will thus normally be implicitly defined by the collection of local views.

The programmer's local view of the database is defined by specifying which DBMOD is to be used when the database is opened. TOTAL is not a CODASYL system, however the function of the DBMOD is similar to that of a CODASYL subschema.

DATA GROUPING

In this section the facilities provided by the five DBMSs for combining basic items of data are defined. Fields can be combined to form group fields. A group field which is allowed to have a number of occurrences is known as a repeating group or a periodic group. Fields and groups are combined to form records which are held in files.

ADABAS

An ADABAS database is defined in terms of (logical) files, records, groups and fields. All of the logical files comprising the database normally reside on one operating system data set or file. The operating system data set is divided into a number of areas which are referred to as ADABAS *files*. These files are identified by a file number. Multi-volume data sets are supported and multiple operating system data sets can be used to support different device types.

Each ADABAS file contains one record type. A record consists of one or more fields. Four field types may be used:

— *Elementary field*. One occurrence of the data-item in each record.

— *Multiple field*. Multiple occurrences of a data-item within each record, ie a vector or array.

— *Group*. One or more adjacent fields can be considered as a group. Elementary fields and/or groups can appear in a group.

— *Periodic group*. A group may itself have multiple occurrences.

Null occurrences of fields do not occupy any physical storage so the physical records are variable in length.

A record has one or more 'DESCRIPTOR' fields defined within it. These fields can be used to formulate search criteria for performing database inquiries. Descriptor fields are key fields which allow the records to be accessed randomly or sequentially. A descriptor field may be an elementary or a multiple field which may be a member of a periodic group. A descriptor may be defined as a part of a field, as a combination of a number of fields or as portions of a number of fields. There may be up to two hundred descriptors per ADABAS (logical) file.

DMS 1100

A DMS 1100 database is defined in terms of areas, records, groups and fields. Each AREA corresponds to an operating system file which may span more than one device. The AREAs of the database define the physical storage available.

The basic addressable unit of data in the database is a RECORD. A database will normally consist of a large number of different record types. Each AREA may contain different record types and a record type may be defined to be eligible to be stored in a number of specified AREAs.

A record comprises one or more FIELDs. The following FIELD types are available:

— *Elementary field*. One occurrence of the data-item in each record.

— *Multiple field*. An array or vector of data-items. The bounds of the array may be fixed or variable.

- *Group field.* One or more fields may be considered as one field. It may contain elementary or multiple fields.

- *Periodic group.* A group field may be repeated a fixed or variable number of times.

A record type may optionally be given a key, termed a CALC field, which may be used to store and retrieve the record.

IDMS

An IDMS database is defined in terms of files, areas, records, groups and fields. The database consists of one or more operating system data sets, or FILES, which define how much physical storage space is available. This space is divided up into one or more units, of user-defined size, called AREAs. A FILE may contain one or more AREAs and an AREA may span more than one FILE.

The basic addressable unit in an IDMS database is a RECORD. Different record types can be defined. Each AREA may contain one or more record types. In some implementations a particular record type can only belong to one AREA. Others allow a record type to belong to more than one AREA.

A RECORD is made up of one or more FIELDS. The following types of fields are permitted:

- *Elementary field.* One occurrence of the data item in each record.

- *Multiple field.* An array or vector of data items. The bounds of the array may be fixed or variable.

- *Group field.* One or more fields can be considered as one field. It may contain elementary or multiple fields.

- *Periodic group.* A group field may be repeated a fixed or variable number of times.

A record type may optionally be given a key, called a CALC field, which can be used to store and retrieve the record.

IMS-DL/1

A DL/1 database is defined in terms of fields, segments and Data Base Descriptions (DBDs). A DBD describes a data structure or database record type. Each data structure contains one or more segment types which are hierarchically related.

There are three types of DBD. A physical DBD defines the structure of a physical database record and the characteristics of the data set (file) that contains it on physical storage. A logical DBD defines a logical database record which consists of selected segment types from one or more physical structures. Finally, an index DBD may be defined for secondary indexing.

A segment is a collection of logically-related data fields. The programmer addresses data at the segment level. A segment may be of fixed or variable length. A field is the smallest unit of information that may be accessed.

TOTAL

A TOTAL database is defined in terms of data sets (files), elements (groups), sub-elements (sub-groups), and items (fields). The database will consist of one or more operating system data sets. Each data set corresponds to one, and only one, TOTAL data set which contains database records. The records on any given data set are of fixed length. A TOTAL database is constructed from two distinct types of data sets: *Master Data Sets* and *Variable Entry Data Sets*. (Master Data Sets are sometimes called *Single Entry Data Sets.)*

A Master Data Set consists of fixed-length records of the same format. Each record has one, and only one, control field or logical key which is used to retrieve the record. This control field must be unique: duplicate record keys are not allowed.

A Variable Entry Data Set consists of fixed-length records but a number of record formats can be specified. Each record may have a number of control fields which are used to access it. The number of control fields may be different for each record format. The control fields in Variable Entry Data Sets are used to link related records to records in a Master Data Set.

A record, irrespective of whether it is part of a Master or Variable Entry Data Set, is defined in terms of *elements, sub-elements* and *items*. A data item (field) is the smallest identifiable and accessible data entry. A data element (group) is a collection of one or more data items. A data element can be further divided into sub-elements (sub-groups or group fields within a group).

LOGICAL RELATIONSHIPS

The logical structuring facilities provided by the five DBMSs are described in this section. The structures supported by each DBMS are summarised diagrammatically. The left-hand columns of these diagrams illustrate the relationships between the record types. A rectangle represents a record type and an arrow a one-to-many relationship. The right-hand column shows a sample occurrence of the relationship. Here the rectangles are record occurrences (the record name is subscripted) and the arrows represent links between the records. The structures illustrated can be combined in order to build more complex data models.

ADABAS

ADABAS supports inter-field and inter-file relationships. Inter-field relationships are simply hierarchical relationships between the fields of a record which are established by the use of periodic groups.

Inter-file relationships are established by using descriptor fields. These fields make it possible to retrieve records from a database file randomly, in the ascending logical sequence of any descriptor, in chronological order or in ascending or descending sequence defined by sorting on up to three descriptor fields. Logical operators may be used to generate complex search criteria involving a number of descriptor fields. Implicit inter-file relationships can therefore be established by application programs. Data retrieved from one file may contain a descriptor value which may be used to retrieve related information from a second file.

ADABAS also supports explicit relationships between files by what is known as *file coupling*. Any two files may be coupled together through a common descriptor field so that descriptors from both files may be used in search criteria. Once a coupling relationship has been established it is automatically maintained by ADABAS. File coupling is normally used to provide high-speed on-line retrieval when using the query language or report writer. Some authorities do not recommend its use in batch environments since the coupling relationship would be bound into the program logic which would make it more difficult to change the database, without program changes, at some future date.

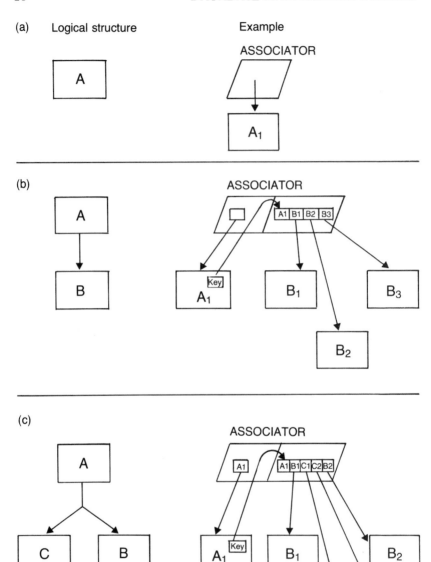

Figure 1   ADABAS Structures

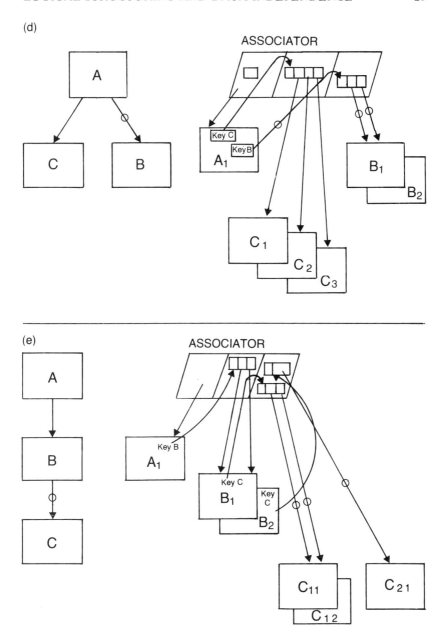

Figure 1 ADABAS Structures (continued)

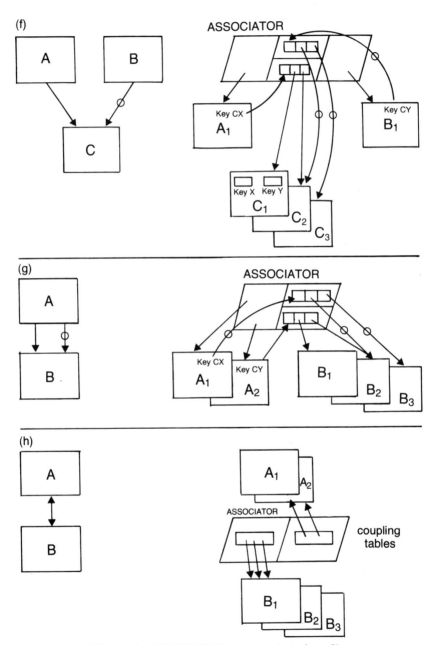

Figure 1   ADABAS Structures (continued)

Utilities are used to add or remove descriptor fields and coupling relationships. This can be done at any time without any need to unload and reload the database. The user therefore has the flexibility of being able to establish relationships as the need arises.

Figure 1 illustrates the basic relationships supported by ADABAS.

DMS 1100

DMS 1100 supports inter-field and inter-record relationships. Inter-area relationships, which are equivalent to inter-file relationships, are supported, but these are logically equivalent to inter-record relationships so no distinction has been made. Inter-field relationships are simply the hierarchical relationships which are established by use of the group fields.

Inter-record relationships are termed SET TYPES. Each set defines a relationship between one record known as the OWNER and zero, one or more records known as MEMBERs. The MEMBERs and OWNER of a SET are related together to establish the relationship. Figure 2 illustrates how this represents a one-to-many relationship and two ways in which it may be implemented. The physical organisation is discussed in the chapter on DBMS Internals.

The records in a set may be linked together in a number of ways. If the records are CHAINed together they are always linked 'NEXT', but 'PRIOR' and/or 'OWNER' linkages may also be specified as illustrated in Figure 3. Alternatively, records in a set may be related by a POINTER ARRAY (Figure 4).

The Set Order, which is specified in the schema, determines where in a set of member records a new entry is to be placed. The five options which are valid for a CHAINed set are described below.

FIRST
   The new member is linked into the set so that it is first on the next chain.

LAST
   The new member is linked into the set so that it is last in the next chain.

NEXT
   The new member is linked into the set immediately following the member record that is currently being used.

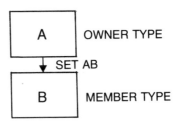

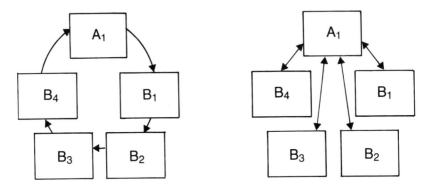

Figure 2   CODASYL Set

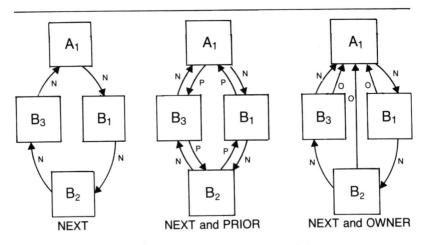

(NEXT, PRIOR and OWNER is also valid)

Figure 3   Chaining Modes

PRIOR

> The new member is linked into the set immediately preceding the member record that is currently being used.

SORTED

> The new member is linked into the set so that the members are in a sorted sequence based on a specified field within the member records. The sort can be in either ASCENDING or DESCENDING sequence and duplicate keys can be either allowed or disallowed.

If the records in a set are related by a POINTER ARRAY (Figure 4), there are two valid set orders:

SORTED BY DATABASE KEY

> The pointer array entries are sorted into ascending sequence by the member records' database keys. A database key identifies the physical location of a record.

SORTED INDEXED BY DEFINED KEYS

> The key is stored in the pointer array and this is used to sort the entries.

When a member of a set is defined it is necessary to specify whether such records will AUTOMATICALLY be linked into the set when they are added to the database. Alternatively, the member records can be described as MANUAL, in which case records added to the database are not linked into the appropriate set; it is left to an application program to do this at some future date. Both AUTOMATIC and MANUAL members may be removed, ie unlinked, from a set in which they participate.

A record type may be defined as INDEX-SEQUENTIAL. In this case an index is constructed and maintained in ascending or descending key sequence. Duplicates may be allowed or not allowed. The records are loaded in their key sequence and arranged physically sequential on the database.

INDEX-SEQUENTIAL and CALC location modes support a primary access key for a record type. Additional access keys can be implemented by indexed pointer array (SORTED INDEXED) sets. Each secondary key corresponds to a singular set occurrence of which the set index forms a secondary index for the required key.

Simple relationships between two record types or one record type and

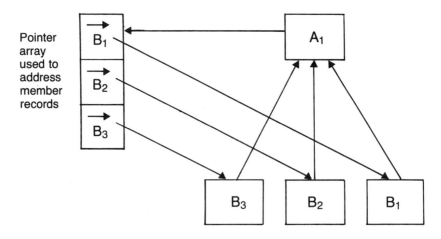

Figure 4   Pointer Array

an index have been used to describe the facilities available in DMS 1100. More complex structures can be constructed using these building blocks. Figure 5 illustrates the basic building blocks.

IDMS

IDMS supports inter-field and inter-record relationships. Inter-area relationships, which are equivalent to inter-field relationships, are also supported but these are very similar to inter-record relationships so no special distinction is necessary. Inter-field relationships are simply hierarchical relationships between the fields of a record which are established by the use of group fields.

Inter-record relationships are called SETS in IDMS. Each set defines a relationship between one record, termed the OWNER, and zero, one or more different records known as MEMBERS. The member records are chained to the OWNER.

The records in a set can be chained together in a number of ways. Records are always linked 'NEXT', but 'PRIOR' and/or 'OWNER' linkages can optionally be specified (see Figure 3).

IDMS allows Set Membership options to be defined in the Schema. Set Membership determines whether it is MANDATORY for a record to be a member of a set or whether this is OPTIONAL. It also determines whether the record should be AUTOMATICally added to the appropriate set when it is added to the database or whether it is to be left unlinked so that it may be MANUALly linked into a set at a later time. The possible Set Membership options are summarised below.

MANDATORY AUTOMATIC
A new member must be a member of a set and it is linked into the set by the system.

OPTIONAL AUTOMATIC
A member need not necessarily be a member of a set but it will be linked to a set by the system when it is first added to the database.

MANDATORY MANUAL
A new member is not linked into a set when it is added but once it is linked into a set it cannot be unlinked.

OPTIONAL MANUAL
A member need not necessarily be a member of a set and will not be linked into a set when it is first added to the database.

The Manual and Automatic options determine what happens when a record is added to the database. The Mandatory and Optional options determine whether a record can be removed from a set.

IDMS also allows the Set Order to be specified in the Schema. Set Order determines where in a set of member records a new entry is to be placed. There are five possibilities namely, FIRST, LAST, NEXT, PRIOR and SORTED, which are summarised below.

FIRST
The new member is linked into the set so that it is first on the NEXT chain.

LAST
The new member is linked into the set so that it is last on the NEXT chain.

NEXT
The new member is linked into the set immediately following the member record that is currently being used.

PRIOR
The new member is linked into the set immediately preceding the member record that is currently being used.

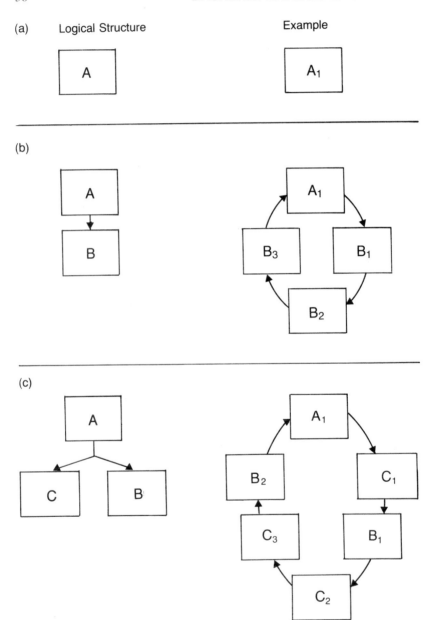

Figure 5   DMS 1100/IDMS Structures

(d)

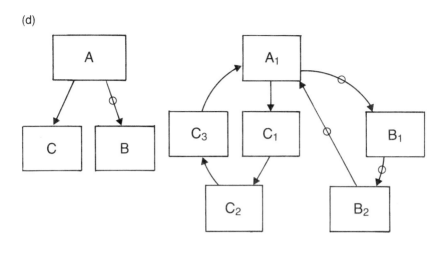

(e)

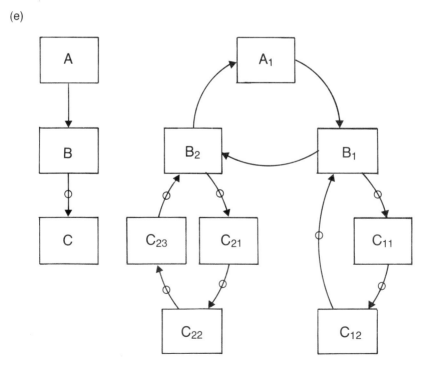

Figure 5   DMS 1100/IDMS Structures (continued)

(f)

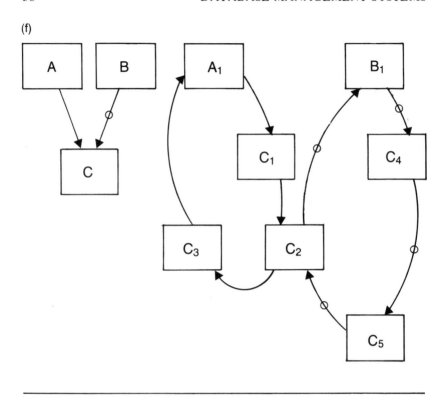

(g)

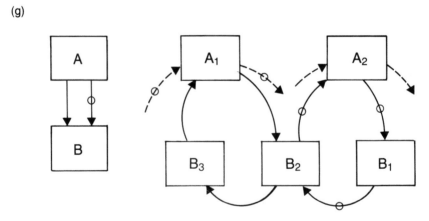

Figure 5   DMS 1100/IDMS Structures (continued)

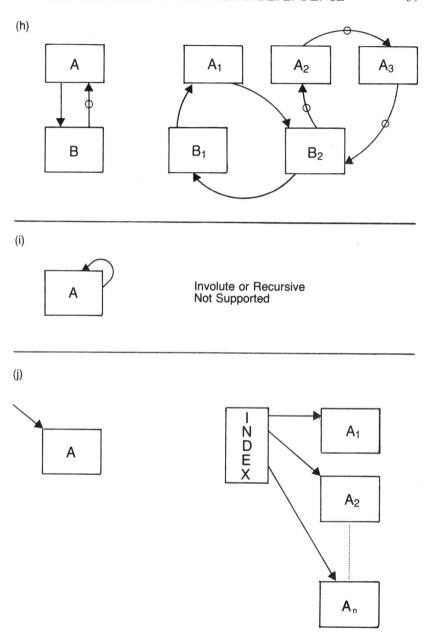

Figure 5   DMS 1100/IDMS Structures (continued)

SORTED

The new member is linked into the set so that the members are in sorted sequence based on a specified field within the member records. The sort can be in either ASCENDING or DESCENDING sequence and duplicate sort keys can be either allowed or not allowed.

A simple relationship between two record types has been used to describe the Set Membership options and the Record Placement modes. Complex data structures can be constructed using the SET concept as illustrated in Figure 5. Some implementations of IDMS allow a set relationship to be built using an index rather than a chain (Figures 2 and 4). Indexes may also be set up to access the records on specified fields or groups of fields.

IMS-DL/1

DL/1 supports inter-segment relationships. Inter-field relationships may be considered to be a form of inter-segment relationship since a conventional group field can be compared with a segment. Inter-record relationships can also be considered as a form of inter-segment relationship since a database record may be viewed as a number of record types, each consisting of a different subset of the segment types in the physical database record. Even an inter-file relationship where a logical database record is defined in terms of segments from different physical databases, and therefore different files, is logically viewed as an inter-segment relationship.

A DL/1 database record consists of one or more segments arranged hierarchically to form an inverted tree structure. Each occurrence of a database record has one, and only one, root segment. The root segment may have zero or more dependent segment types.

The basic construct used to create a hierarchical structure is the parent/child relationship between segment types. A segment type at one level in the hierarchy may be the parent of one or more children segment types in the next lower level of the hierarchy. The relationship between the parent segment and any given child segment type is always one-to-many (ie 1 to 0, 1 or more). Multiple occurrences of a segment type are termed twins. A child segment may itself be a parent, as shown in Figure 6.

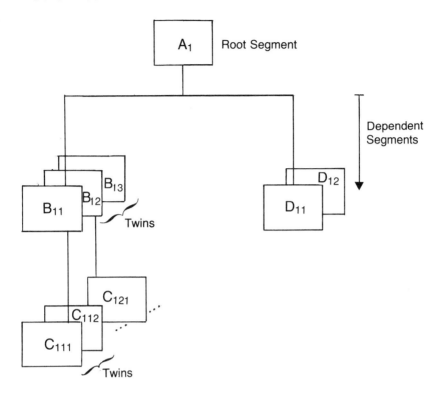

A is the parent of B and D

B and D are children of A

B is the parent of C

C is the child of B

B_{11}, B_{12}, B_{13} are twins

C_{111}, C_{112} are twins

Figure 6   A DL/1 Hierarchy

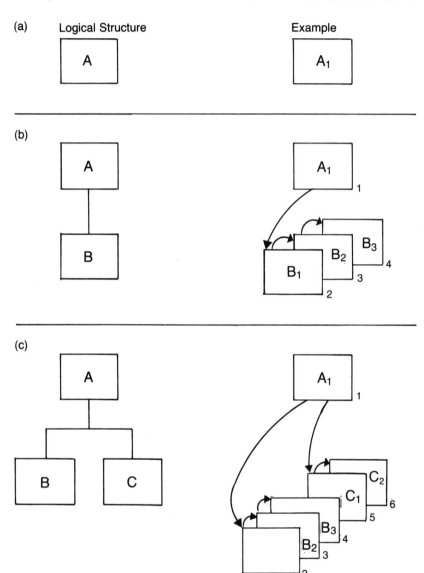

Figure 7   DL/1 Structures

(d)

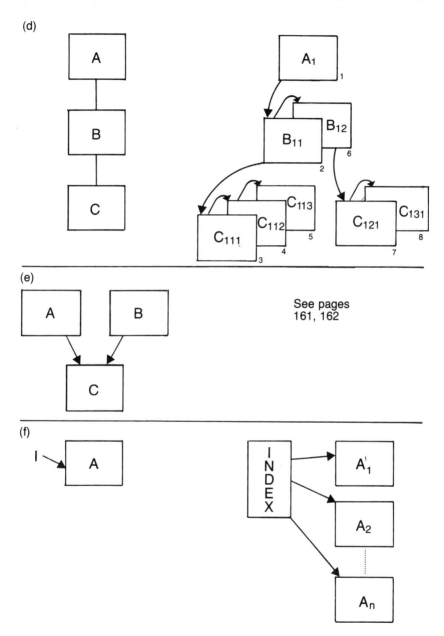

(e)

See pages
161, 162

(f)

Figure 7   DL/1 Structures (continued)

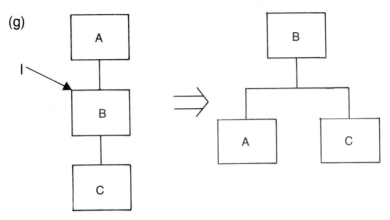

Figure 7   DL/1 Structures (continued)

When logical relationships are constructed, two sets of design rules must be observed. One set specifies the rules for defining logical relationships in the physical databases, ie the physical DBD. The second set specifies the rules for defining the logical databases, ie the logical DBD.

Unidirectional relationships, bidirectional relationships and secondary indexing may be used to establish inter-segment relations. However, these are just different ways of implementing the logical view so they are discussed in the chapter 'Internals'. The logical view of the data is always a hierarchy of segments. Figure 7 illustrates the basic structures and the order in which segments are accessed when the structure is read serially.

When a DBD is defined, segment insertion rules are specified. A new segment may be inserted so that it is logically the first or last child of its parent. Alternatively, a new segment may be inserted after the child that is currently being processed by the program. If a segment type has a sequence field (key) its occurrences are ordered in ascending key sequence, duplicates being placed after other occurrences with the same key.

TOTAL

TOTAL supports inter-field, inter-file and inter-record relationships. Inter-field relationships are simply hierarchical relationships between fields of a record which are established by the use of elements and sub-elements (group fields).

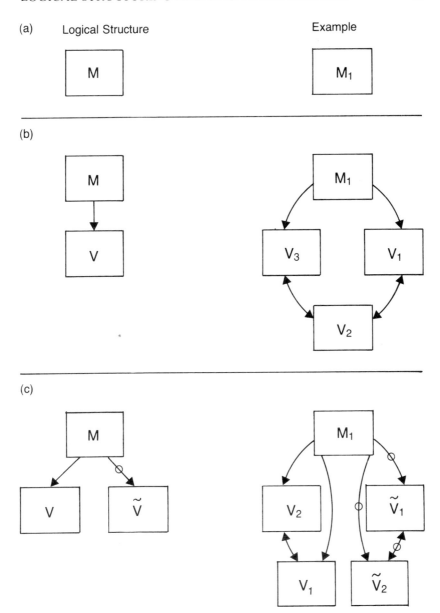

Figure 8   TOTAL Structures

(d)

(e)

(f)

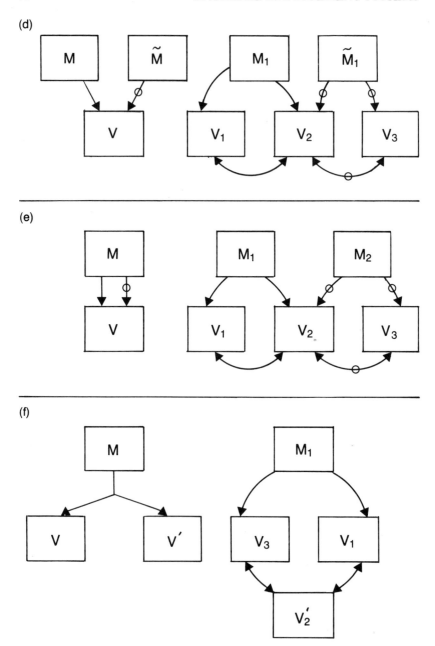

Figure 8　TOTAL Structures (continued)

(g)

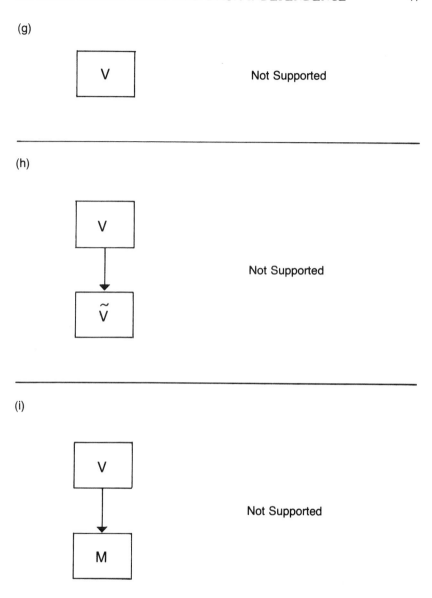

Figure 8   TOTAL Structures (continued)

Inter-file relationships can be established between two or more Master Data Sets. The control key allows one record in a Master Data Set to be accessed. If this record is used to store control keys for one or more Master Data Sets then implicit inter-file relationships can be programmed which relate two or more Master Data Sets together.

Inter-record relationships can be established between records in Master Data Sets and those in Variable Data Sets. A record in a Master Data Set may be considered to be the owner of one or more sets of records. Each set of records must consist of records of the same type. All records of a given type must belong to only one Variable Entry Data Set, but each type could belong to a different Variable Entry Data Set.

Variable Entry Data Sets can only be accessed via a Master Data Set. Related records within a Variable Entry Data Set are linked together by next and prior pointers which have a Master Data Set record at the head of the chain. The chain of pointers is known as a LINKAGE PATH. A number of linkage paths may exist. A Variable Entry record always holds the control key of every Master record that owns it, as well as the next and prior pointers associated with each relationship in which it participates. The various logical structures which may be constructed using these facilities are illustrated in Figure 8.

DATA INDEPENDENCE AND BINDING

This section describes the data independence facilities of the five DBMSs. It defines the level at which data is addressed: for example, some systems allow addressing at the field level, others at the record level. The descriptions also explain how binding is performed.

ADABAS

When a data transfer request is made to the system it is necessary to quote the file number containing the data, the field name and the field format used by the program. A field is therefore only locked to a particular file at the database design stage.

Application programs are independent of the database record layout since a field is identified by its name, not by its relative position in the record. It is possible to add fields and delete those which are not referenced by an application, without affecting application programs.

Application programs are independent of the physical storage mechanism used by the software. The access method and physical structure of the data are transparent to them. In addition, the program is independent of the format and size of a field. ADABAS will, if necessary, convert data from the format used to physically store the data to the format requested by the program. Logical relationships may be added and deleted provided that they are not used by the application system.

ADABAS also supports a high-level Macro INTerface called ADAMINT. ADAMINT macros are used to tailor a 'userview' of the database for an application. Application programs CALL the userview module which handles the ADABAS CALL protocols. This simplifies the interface between the program and the database.

Binding of the program's data requirements to the data in physical storage occurs at run time. At run time the program identifies to the software which files, fields within the files and data formats are to be used. The logical relationships will be assumed by the programs and will have effectively been bound at the design stage.

Some data independence may be lost through the use of group fields. If a group field is used within a program the fields within the group are bound at program compile time. Such database fields cannot be altered without affecting the programs which use the group.

DMS 1100

DMS 1100 transfers data to and from application programs on a record basis. In DMS 1100 terminology a logical file is termed an AREA. A given record type may be held on one or more AREAs. A record type is *not* therefore bound to one AREA at the design stage.

The subschema may present the program with just the fields actually required, ie a subset of the complete record. Fields not included in the program's subschema view of the record may be added, changed and deleted without affecting it. The subschema therefore makes application programs independent of the physical layout of record types. If a subschema is used which presents the whole record to the program and some change to the format is required then every program referencing the record type may need to be modified.

DMS 1100 supports a 'CHECK' facility which allows, amongst other things, the format of data to be verified for either the whole record, or selected fields.

The physical organisation and physical access method are transparent to the programmer. The subschema may convert data items from the physical representation into formats supported by the host language if the host language does not support the Schema definition of the data. Record layouts, complete with their description of the data, are copied into the program by the DML preprocessor.

Logical relationships may be removed from the Schema without affecting applications that do not use them. New relationships may be added without affecting existing applications provided that they do not impose constraints on the existing database structure.

A program's data requirements are bound to the data in physical storage partly at program compile time and partly at run time. At compile time the relative positions of the fields within the subschema view of the record types are bound to the program. At run time the physical data is mapped to the program by the subschema.

Logical relationships used by the programs will have effectively been bound at the design stage.

Some data independence may be lost through the use of group fields. If a group field is referenced by a program, the fields within the group are effectively bound to the program at compile time. Fields within such a group cannot be altered without modifying every program which uses them.

IDMS

IDMS transfers data to and from an application program on a record basis. The programmer must specify, either explicitly or implicitly, which logical IDMS file the record is in. Some implementations only allow a record type to belong to one logical file, known as an AREA in IDMS terminology, in which case the record is locked to a particular AREA at the design stage.

As IDMS transfers records rather than individual fields of data, the program will be sensitive to the record format. If a subschema is used which transfers the whole record, and it is necessary to change the record in some way then every program using it will need to be modified.

Alternatively, a subschema which only transfers the fields required by a program can be used. In this case fields can be added, changed and deleted without affecting those programs which do not use those being modified.

Programs are independent of the physical storage mechanism used by IDMS. However, IDMS does not check or convert the contents of a data field. The programmer does not need to be concerned with the physical format of the data. The record layout, defining the attributes of each field (ie length and format), is copied into the program from a 'Directory' by the preprocessor.

Existing logical relationships can be deleted without affecting applications that do not use them. Logical relationships may be added without affecting existing applications if they do not impose constraints on the existing database structure.

A program's data requirements are bound to the data in physical storage partly at program compile time and partly at run time. At program compile time the relative positions of the fields within a record and the field formats are bound to the program. At run time the physical data is mapped to the program by the subschema. The logical relationships are assumed by the programs so they are effectively bound at the program design stage.

Some data independence may be lost through the use of group fields. When a group field is referenced by a program the fields within the group are bound to the program at compile time. The fields within such a group cannot be altered without modifying the programs that use them.

IMS-DL/1

DL/1 transfers segments of data to and from application programs. The Program Specification Block used by a program specifies which segments in the physical or logical database may be accessed. A program may use a 'Segment Search Argument' (discussed in Chapter 5) to select only those segments of interest.

Data independence is therefore provided down to the segment level. The format of any segments which are not used by the program may be changed without having any effect on the program. However, the position of a segment within a record hierarchy cannot necessarily be changed without modifying any programs which are sensitive to it.

Field Level Sensitivity allows application programs to access an ordered subset of the fields contained in a segment. Data independence is therefore available down to a field level. The order of the fields within a segment may be changed if required. Fields may be added or fields which are not referenced may be deleted without affecting the application programs using the segment.

Programs are, in general, independent of the way in which the data is physically stored. The access method used to address the data and the physical structure of the data are transparent to the programmer. However, the programmer must be familiar with the formats of the segments accessed, ie the position, length and format of the data fields. If the Field Level Sensitivity facility is used the format of the ordered subset must be known. The format of data loaded into a data field is not validated.

New logical relations may be added to the database without affecting existing programs. Existing logical relationships can be deleted without affecting applications that do not make use of them. A program's data requirements are bound to the data in physical storage partly at program compile time and partly at run time. At compile time the relative positions of the fields within a segment (or ordered subset of fields if the Field Level Sensitivity facility is used) and the field formats are bound to the program. At run time the system accesses the required segments (or subsets of them) without being dependent upon changes to unreferenced segments.

The logical relationships will be assumed by the application programs and will have effectively been bound at the program design stage. When the database is designed the data may be bound to a particular access method. Normally it is possible to change the physical access method used by a Data Base Definition without altering the logical structure of the database.

TOTAL

When a data transfer request is made to TOTAL, the programmer has to quote the file name containing the data and the names of the fields of interest. A field is therefore locked to a particular file when the database is designed. Application programs are independent of the database record layout since a field is identified by name, not by its relative position within the record. It is therefore possible to add new fields to the record type and delete those which are not referenced without affecting applications. An application program will only need to be maintained if a change to the database affects one or more of the fields used by the program.

Programs are independent of the physical storage mechanism and access method used by TOTAL. The programmer must, however, know the physical attributes of a data field, ie the length and format. TOTAL does not check or convert the contents of a data field.

New logical relationships may be added to the database without affecting the data independence of existing applications. Existing logical relationships can be removed without affecting applications that do not make use of them. A program's data requirements are bound to the data in physical storage at run time. At this time the program identifies which files and fields within the files are to be used. Strictly speaking the binding of fields can occur at command execution time. A program passes TOTAL an 'item list' which lists the field names required in the order to be used by the program. This list can be interpreted every time a command is executed or just once to avoid the overhead of reinterpreting them every time they are used.

The logical relationships used by the programs will have effectively been bound at design time. The attributes of the data fields, ie their lengths and format, are also bound at the design stage.

Some data independence may be lost if group fields (known as *data elements* in TOTAL's terminology) are used. When a group field is used within a program, the fields within the group are bound to the program at compile time. Such fields cannot be altered without affecting the programs which use them.

3 Security and Integrity

The objectives of this chapter are to:

— discuss the need for security and integrity facilities in a DBMS;

and for each of the five DBMSs to:

— describe the backup, recovery and restart facilities;

— discuss the features for controlling access to the data;

— consider what data validation is performed on the data;

— explain how the DBMS manages a number of programs which are concurrently accessing the database.

INTRODUCTION

The data which an organisation holds on its database is of great value. In fact, an organisation's existence may rely on the continuing availability of its data. Consider, for example, the consequences of the irrecoverable destruction of an insurance company's database. The company would not have a record of its customers, the policies they hold, their claim history, etc. It is, in fact, unlikely that the company could continue in business.

Obviously, organisations must ensure that up-to-date copies of all the data essential for the running of their business are taken at regular intervals. This applies not only to the database but also to other computer files and data held in filing cabinets.

The time taken to recover a lost or damaged database may be critical to an organisation's business. For example, if an on-line airline reservation system was out of action for a few days, the airline's business would be seriously affected.

The database, or parts of it, could be lost as a result of a hardware or software failure. For example, a disk holding part of the database could become unusable or a rogue program could overwrite some of the files comprising the database. Fortunately losses of this kind are not likely to occur frequently.

On the other hand, there is a risk that the database may be damaged every time it is updated. As a consequence of an update program failing, the database could be left in an inconsistent state. Consider, for example, a program transferring money from a deposit account to a current account which fails after debiting the deposit account but before crediting the current account. In this example only a few fields of data will be in error. However, if the DBMS was updating the pointers or indexes used to implement the data structures, the effects cóuld be more serious. Certain records could become inaccessible or the wrong records could be retrieved in response to a retrieval request. In both cases the integrity of the database has been lost. In order to cope with the problems discussed above, most DBMSs provide a number of facilities for securing a database and maintaining its integrity. There are three types of facility:

— *Backup*. Utilities provided with the DBMS or the operating system are used to take a copy of the database. If the need arises this copy can be restored and the database brought up-to-date by rerunning any applications which have been run since the backup was taken. Backup copies will need to be taken regularly enough to avoid the need to rerun an excessive number of programs. This approach is clearly unsatisfactory if on-line updating is taking place.

When backups, also called dumps, are taken it is essential to ensure that all the physical database files which are linked in any way, perhaps by an index or pointer chains, are copied at the same time otherwise the dumps will prove useless.

— *Recovery/Restart*. The DBMS maintains a log (sometimes called a *journal* or *audit trail*) of all the changes made to the database. Usually, a before and after copy (or 'image') of every updated record is taken. In the event of a failure the logged copies of the updated records can be used to recover the database. DBMS utilities allow the 'before images' to be restored thereby removing the effects of a failed program. Alternatively, the 'after images' can be applied to a restored backup copy in order to bring it up-to-date thereby removing the need to rerun many hours of application programs. Clearly, all the logs produced since the last backup must be available.

This type of facility significantly reduces recovery time but on-line updates still pose a problem.

— *Automatic Recovery or Rollback.* This approach is a natural development of the one above. The before images of an active update program are held on a disk file. If the program fails, the DBMS automatically copies back its before images. When an update program successfully completes processing, its before images can either be thrown away or placed on the log for possible future use as described above in Recovery/Restart. This approach is ideal for on-line transaction programs.

Besides protecting the data from accidental or malicious loss or damage, the DBMS should also offer facilities to allow access to the data to be controlled. Anybody who uses the database should not necessarily be allowed to retrieve, change or delete anything on it. The data may be of value to a competitor or it may be of a private and confidential nature.

Management needs to be able to specify which records and fields within those records a user, or group of users, is allowed to see. In addition they should be able to specify whether a user is only allowed to retrieve data or whether modifications and deletions are permitted. Even if management decides that access controls are currently unnecessary the situation may change in the future. For example, future privacy legislation may make controls necessary, or management may change its mind after being the victim of a fraud or industrial espionage.

The data in a database is usually shared by a number of applications. Such sharing does not present any problems if all the programs only retrieve data. However, if some of the programs update the database two types of data inconsistency may arise:

— *Retrieval Inconsistency.* This can happen, for example, if a retrieval program accesses a record twice but between these two accesses the record is updated by some other program. The integrity of the database has not been destroyed, but the retrieval program may produce some strange results because the programmer wrongly assumed that none of the data could change while the program was running.

— *Update Inconsistency*. This occurs if two update programs each
obtain their own copy of the same record. Suppose one program
updates its copy of the record and writes it back to the database
and then the other program does likewise. The first program's
update has been lost. The integrity of the database has also been
lost.

All the DBMSs prevent update inconsistencies but some rely on the
programmer's knowledge to prevent retrieval inconsistencies. The
DBMSs use various 'locking', or record holding strategies in order to
control multiple user access.

BACKUP, RECOVERY AND RESTART

This section describes the backup, recovery and restart facilities supported by the five DBMSs. An installation should plan its use of backups,
logs and automatic rollback facilities very carefully. In general, batch only
systems should use the backup copies and the log (journal/data protection
file/audit trail) to repair a damaged database. The automatic rollback
facilities are ideal for on-line programs but they are likely to prove
expensive to run, in terms of machine resources, for large batch update
programs.

ADABAS

ADABAS has an 'AUTOBACKOUT' capability which automatically
backs out partially completed transactions. A work file is used to store
information about active logical transactions. A logical transaction is a
series of commands which must be completed in order to ensure that the
database is consistent from an application program point of view.

If the application program fails, ADABAS will backout any updates
applied by a logical transaction which has not been completed. A transaction time limit is used to detect a program which has failed. Completion of
a logical transaction is signalled to the system by the programmer after an
update sequence. An entire program can be considered as a logical
transaction if necessary. The programmer may request the system to
backout the current transaction and continue processing normally.

If an ADABAS session is terminated abnormally, possibly because of a
hardware failure, any incomplete logical transactions will be backed out
when the session is restarted.

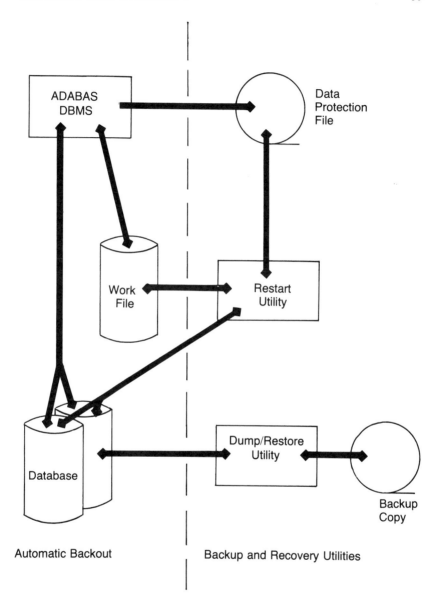

Figure 9   ADABAS Backup and Recovery

When a program signals the end of a logical transaction it may also store data about that transaction. A command is provided which allows the data stored at the end of the last completed logical transaction to be read. This allows programs to be written so that they can automatically restart at the correct point.

A Dump-Restore utility and a Restart utility are provided to control and manage the database. The Dump-Restore utility is used to copy the whole database, or individual files, to and from tape or disk. It is possible to run the dump utility while the database is being updated; the Data Protection File is used to bring the restored copy up-to-date.

The Restart utility is used to repair a damaged database. The BACK-OUT option uses the Data Protection File to backout updates made to a file by restoring the 'before' images. The REGENERATE option uses the Data Protection File to re-apply updates to a file after a backup copy of the file has been restored. The file is regenerated up to a specified checkpoint by restoring the 'after' images.

The backup and recovery facilities of ADABAS are summarised in Figure 9.

DMS 1100

DMS 1100 supports logging, usually referred to as *Looks*. There are three types of Looks, BEFORE LOOKS, AFTER LOOKS and QUICK-BEFORE LOOKS. The first two types are written to an Audit Trail tape and the third type is written to a random access file. Before and Quick-Before Looks are copies of a database page before it was changed in some way. After Looks are copies of a database page after it has been changed. A run-unit will only cause one Before or Quick-Before Look of a given page to be recorded. However multiple After Looks of a given page may be recorded if it is changed a number of times and the buffer is flushed between changes. In order to reduce the volume of data handled, compacted After Looks, which are at the Record rather than the Page level, are written to the Audit Trail. Where possible multiple Looks are buffered into one audit trail block.

The types of *Looks* required are specified for each Area in the schema. Any combination of the three types of Looks is possible or 'NO-LOOKS' can be specified. The DML command 'LOG' allows user data to be written to the Audit Trail by run-units authorised to do so.

When Quick-Before Looks are specified for an area the system will automatically rollback any changes made to the area by a run-unit which fails to terminate normally. The system restores the copies of the pages taken before any changes were made to the database. They are also written to the audit file to nullify the change. If the operating system or machine should fail, DMS 1100 will rollback any run-units that were active at the time of the failure when it is restarted.

The Quick-Before Looks are retained until the run-unit signs off (DEPART) or until a commit point implied by the use of a FREE command. A run-unit may explicitly request to be rolled back by the system.

A higher performance alternative to Quick-Before Looks is provided by 'Deferred Updates'. This works by buffering the updates until the run-unit DEPARTs or signals a commit point. The I/O overhead of quick looks is thereby avoided.

An operating system utility is used for taking backup security copies (or dumps) of the database. Each area is held on an operating system file so they may be dumped and restored selectively.

Static or Dynamic Dumps may be taken. A Static Dump is taken when no run-units are updating the areas being dumped. A Dynamic Dump allows concurrent dumping and updating of the areas being dumped. Possible inconsistencies in the dynamic dump are resolved by use of the audit trail.

A utility is provided to assist in 'Long Recovery' which may be necessary if part of the database is damaged. The damaged part of the database is first restored from a security dump. The utility then processes the audit trail tape in order to bring the restored area(s) up-to-date. The utility restores the After Looks belonging to the area concerned. Recovery can be to a specified recovery point, a specified checkpoint or to the time of the failure. Undamaged parts of the database remain available for normal processing during this operation.

If both Before and After Looks are available it is possible to apply the After Looks up to a specified recovery point, checkpoint or time of failure and then backout any run-units active at the recovery point using the Before Looks. Figure 10 summarises the recovery and backup facilities provided by DMS 1100.

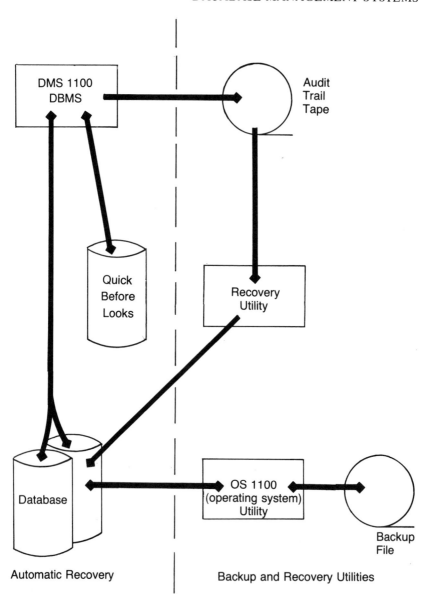

Figure 10   DMS 1100 Backup and Recovery

The duplex file feature of the operating system enables DMS 1100 to optionally maintain duplicate copies of one or more areas. This allows service to be maintained in the event of the loss of one copy due, for example, to a device failure.

IDMS

IDMS optionally supports journalling to either a tape or disk files. Disk journalling uses multiple disk files so that logging may be switched to another file while the full file is cleared. Both disk and tape journalling may be used together although in this situation the tape file is termed an *archive* tape.

All journalling is performed at the Record level with both before and after images before being recorded. Journalled records are buffered for efficiency. A journal block is only written when this is necessary to preserve the system's ability to maintain integrity.

Disk journalling allows IDMS to automatically rollback a failed run-unit. This means that any update made since the run-unit started processing or since its last COMMIT checkpoint is removed from the database. Similarly, if the database software, operating system or machine fails for any reason, IDMS will automatically rollback any incomplete or non-COMMITed processing made by the run-units active at the time of the failure. A run-unit may also request itself to be rolled back by the system.

Journal data is retained in the disk journals until the updates have been COMMITed or the run-unit ends normally. This journal data then becomes eligible for transfer to the journal tape when the journal clear utility is next executed. The journal clear utility only transfers data to the journal tape when it will no longer be required for a possible automatic rollback.

Dump and Restore utilities are provided for taking backup copies of the database, and producing reports, on an Area basis. Another utility is provided to copy the disk journal data to a tape journal.

Three recovery utilities are provided for processing the tape journal. One of these reads the tape, printing details of checkpoints in order to close it since this may not have been done if the system failed. The other two perform rollback and rollforward respectively. The rollback utility uses the before images to backout changes to the database. The rollfor-

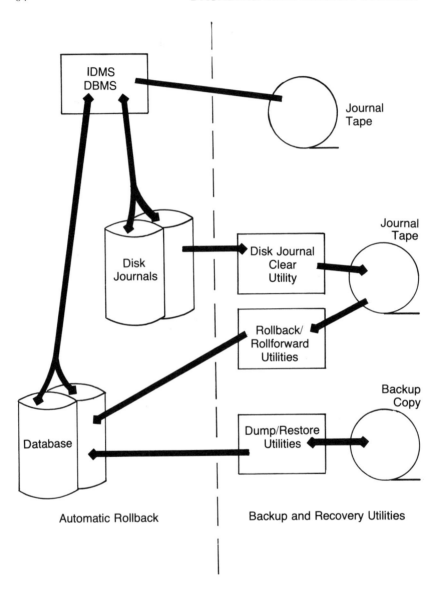

Figure 11   IDMS (Cullinane) Backup and Recovery

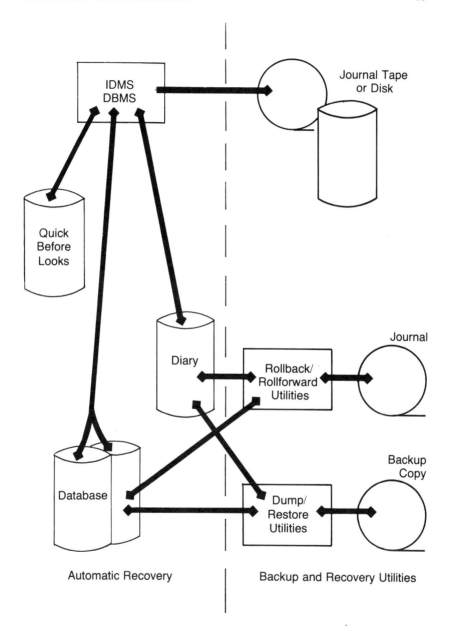

Figure 12   IDMS (ICL) Backup and Recovery

ward utility allows the after images to be applied to a database which has been restored from a security dump.

Some implementations (ICL versions) incorporate a file called the DIARY which is used to record database activity. The DIARY is used to record the following information: Service Start up/Close down details; Application Start/End times; Utility runs; Rollforward and Rollback details. This information is used to co-ordinate recovery and restart.

Some implementations also optionally allow a Quick-Before Looks (QBL) File to be allocated to each updating run-unit. This file is used to hold the unCOMMITed before images of updated records. If the run-unit fails these before images are restored to the database (and written to the main Journal as after images in case this is later used to recover the database). The DIARY is used to co-ordinate the rollback. When Quick-Before Looks are used, the main journal only needs to record after images, rather than before and after images, for offline recovery purposes.

In Service Dumping is also possible in some ICL implementations. An In Service Dump will be logically inconsistent if the areas dumped were being updated. When such a dump is restored the rollforward utility is used to apply any updates performed during the dumps. The DIARY is used to co-ordinate all backup and recovery operations. They also support Duplex database and Journals. It is also possible to have Area Journals to avoid the possible bottleneck of a single Journal.

The backup and recovery features of the Cullinane and ICL versions of IDMS are summarised in Figures 11 and 12 respectively.

IMS-DL/1

DL/1's logging facilities allow log data to be written to a disk or tape log file. Both before and after images of all segments changed by an application program are recorded. The logged records are buffered for efficiency. A block is only written to the log file when this is necessary to allow recovery. Write ahead logging is normally used, ie the logged data is written to the log before the buffers are rewritten to the database. Batch programs running a local copy of DL/1 may use asynchronous logging, which does not synchronise the log writes, in order to improve performance.

Automatic Backout of a failed program is only supported for IMS/DC

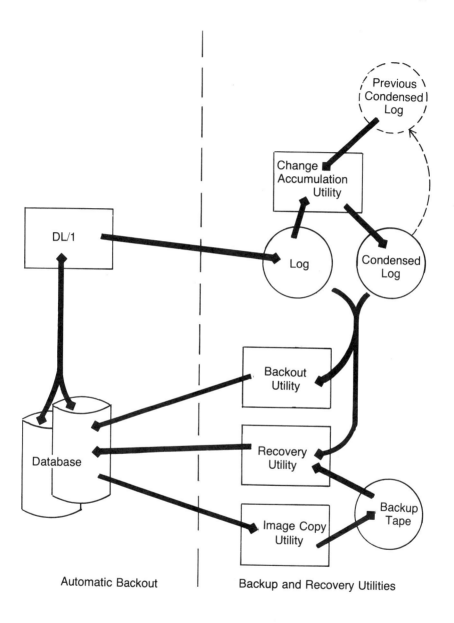

Figure 13   DL/1 Backup and Recovery

and CICS/VS transactions. The on-line system's recovery facilities are used to implement automatic backout. The teleprocessing system and DL/1 share the same log file so that database recovery may be co-ordinated with the recovery of other resources such as non-database files.

A number of utilities are provided for backing up and recovering a database. The Database Data Set Image Copy utility creates a backup copy (normally on tape) of a physical database. A Database Change Accumulation utility processes the log file(s) and possibly the most recent 'condensed log file' to produce a (new) condensed log file. Records produced before a specified date and time or written by the teleprocessing system may be eliminated. All the changes for a given file are grouped together in the correct sequence.

The Database Data Set Recovery utility makes use of the Image Copy backup to recover (part of) the database. The condensed log (Accumulated Change Data Set) and/or log are used to bring the Image Copy of the database up-to-date by applying the after images. A Database Backout utility allows changes made by program(s) to be backed out to a checkpoint or to the start of the program(s). Before images from the log(s) are restored to the database. A new log file is created to reflect the restored state of the database for use in possible future recovery operations.

Figure 13 summarises the backup and recovery features supported by DL/1.

TOTAL

An optional logging facility is provided in TOTAL. The log may be a disk or a tape file. Logging is performed at the record level and logged data is blocked for efficiency. A block of log data is only written when it is full or if it is necessary in order to maintain recovery integrity.

The system allows before, after or both before and after record images to be recorded. Batch programs specify their requirements in the SINON request. When the central version is used the logging options are specified when the system is started.

Special control commands are available for using the log. A program may force a quiesce point (QUIET) in order to synchronise the database

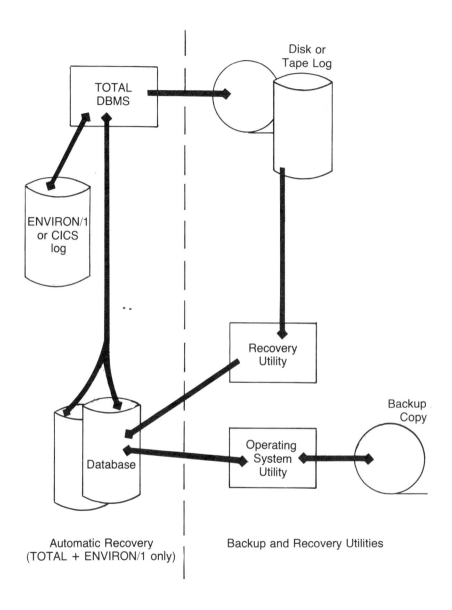

Figure 14   TOTAL Backup and Recovery

with the log to produce a recovery checkpoint. User data may also be written to the log (MARKL).

When TOTAL is run under ENVIRON/1 or CICS, a TP disk log file is supported to provide automatic rollback of failed transactions. The before images of active transactions are recorded on this log. These before images are used to rollback any transaction which fails. Such a transaction is either rolled back completely or, if 'COMIT' checkpoints have been taken, to the latest COMITed point.

Automatic rollback of failed batch programs is not supported. A utility is provided which uses the log file to recover the database. The before images can be used to roll out the effects of a failed program. The after images can be used to bring a restored security copy of the database up-to-date. The utility allows the database to be rolled backward or forward to a specified checkpoint.

The log file may also be processed by user-written programs. Such a program could make use of user data which may be logged to implement a sophisticated recovery.

Operating system file dump and restore utilities are used to take security copies of the TOTAL files. The backup and recovery facilities supported by TOTAL are summarised in Figure 14.

CONTROLLING ACCESS

The facilities provided by the five DBMSs for controlling access to the database are described below. It is interesting to compare the security facilities available under conventional file management with those offered by DBMSs. The access control facilities for conventional files, where they exist at all, only allow access to the file as a whole to be controlled. Under a DBMS, control can be down to the record or even field level and some systems even allow access to be restricted to records satisfying specified conditions.

ADABAS

ADABAS provides access control facilities at the file, field, record and data level. When a program signs on using the High Level DML (ADAMINT) or opens a file using the Low Level DML a password must be provided. The password is checked by ADABAS and converted into a File Profile. This profile defines the read and the update authorisation levels assigned to the password for each file.

If an invalid password is given, or if the programmer is attempting to use a file not authorised by the password, the sign-on or open request is rejected and any subsequent ADABAS requests are also rejected. Details of the attempted access can be recorded on a statistics file so that the Data Base Administrator may take appropriate action. An error response code is returned to the program.

Field-level access control is implemented by assigning each field a pair of Security Levels, one for access and one for update. The File Profile defines, for each file, the pair of Permission Levels associated with the password. A command is only processed if the Permission Level is greater than or equal to the Security Level. Only authorised personnel may access and maintain the File Profile.

Record-level access control makes use of a facility called Security by Value. The value of a field within the database record is used to determine whether information from the record can be accessed or updated. The DBA defines, for each password that permits access to the file, a list of values that the field must contain for access to be granted.

ADABAS also has a ciphering feature which provides access control at the data level. A cipher key can be used to 'scramble' the data so that a dump of memory or external storage would be unintelligible. The data can only be 'unscrambled' by providing the system with the correct cipher key. When ciphering is used one cipher key is used for all the fields within ·a ciphered file.

DMS 1100

DMS 1100 provides control facilities at the schema, subschema, area, set, record and field levels. An ACCESS CONTROL clause can be specified at all of these levels. This clause allows either a password to be specified or a DBA written procedure to be called to determine whether access is to be permitted.

The subschema used by a program determines which database components may be accessed and how they may be used. Use of the ACCESS CONTROL clause in the schema allows unauthorised use of a subschema to be prevented.

At the AREA level the ACCESS CONTROL clause allows the usage mode of an AREA, specified in a run-unit's OPEN command, to be controlled. The usage mode specifies whether the AREA is to be used for RETRIEVAL or UPDATE and whether other run-units may concurrently access it. Access to a set and manipulation of manual members may be controlled by specifying an ACCESS CONTROL clause in the set definition.

An ACCESS CONTROL clause at the record level allows the use of DML commands which access, update or manipulate the records to be controlled. Procedures may also be specified which perform ENCODING and DECODING of the entire record. Such procedures could be used for compressing and decompressing a record.

At the field level the ACCESS CONTROL clause allows access (FETCH, GET) and modification (STORE, MODIFY) of individual data fields to be controlled. A field can also be ENCODED and DECODED.

IDMS

IDMS provides access control facilities at the program, area, set and record level. Most of these facilities are specified within the subschema. The subschema used by a program determines which elements of the database may be accessed and how they may be accessed. It is therefore necessary for the DBA to be able to specify which subschema each program may use. A facility in the directory allows a list of program and subschema names to be registered so that a program may only be preprocessed successfully if the correct subschema is specified. This list also provides useful documentation and prevents rogue, unregistered programs being preprocessed.

When the subschema is coded PRIVACY LOCKS may be specified for each area, set and record. Currently these locks either allow or disallow use of facilities to all users of the subschema. There is no password checking mechanism.

There are no privacy locks at the field level. However a program can be presented with a subset of the physical record. The program's view of the record is specified in the subschema by naming the fields which are to be presented to the program.

IDMS also supports database procedures which can be used to implement security and access controls. The name of user-written procedures may be included in the Area and Record Description sections of the Schema DDL. These procedures allow user specified checks to be carried out before a DML verb is processed, after it has been completed and when an error condition occurs.

IMS-DL/1

DL/1 provides access control facilities at the physical database (file) and segment level. When a physical DBD is defined the VSAM data sets used to implement it can optionally be password protected. The DBD name is used as the password so DL/1 can always access the data sets without prompting for a password. This facility prevents non DL/1 programs from accessing the database 'accidentally'.

Segment-level access is controlled by the PSB. The PSB defines a program's local view of the database. Only the segments defined in the PCBs (which are held in the PSB) may be accessed; the program is said to be 'sensitive' to these segments. Segment Processing Options allow the way in which each individual segment may be accessed to be controlled. These indicate whether a program may Get, Insert, Replace or Delete a segment type. There are also a number of exits which allow the authority of a user to access the data to be checked.

If the field-level sensitivity feature is used the DBA may specify which fields within a segment can be accessed and whether they can be updated.

When an illegal access attempt is detected an appropriate response code is returned to the program. The Performance Monitoring Utility of IMS/VS can produce a DL/1 Call Summary which may be used by the DBA to investigate access violations.

TOTAL

TOTAL provides access control at the file and field level. When a programs signs on to TOTAL it must identify which 'DBMOD' is to be used. This Data Base Module defines the program's view of the database. Only the files described in this view may be accessed.

Field-level access control can be implemented by only supplying the programmer with the names of the fields that are required by the application. Since the programmer has to identify the fields required by name any fields whose names are unknown are secure from access. A greater degree of security could be obtained by generating a DBMOD which uses dummy names (defined as *FILLER* in the DBDL) for secure fields. Then, even programmers who know the correct names cannot access them with the DBMOD in use.

The TOTAL software optionally includes the 'skeleton' of an access control program. An installation wishing to implement security controls may tailor this program to meet their needs. The 'skeleton' program is implemented as an interface between the application program and the TOTAL nucleus. The application program provides a password on the first 'CALL' which is used as a Control Key to access a record on a TOTAL file. This record can contain data to validate the application program's right of access.

DATA VALIDATION

This section describes what checks, if any, are made on the data by the five DBMSs in order to prevent meaningless data being written to the database. Any form of data validation performed by the DBMS can be valuable since it can help to maintain the integrity of the data by stopping programs erroneously storing invalid data. A program may, for example, try to add a new record which contains some uninitialised fields. Once invalid data gets onto the database it may be difficult to detect and correct it.

'Group moves' and group redefinition can cause data of the wrong format to be loaded into a database record area. The code generated by the compiler has no way of verifying that the data moved into a field has the correct internal format (binary, floating point, etc). Any programs which subsequently use the data will either fail or interpret the data wrongly and produce erroneous results.

ADABAS

When a new record is to be added to the database or a field has been updated ADABAS verifies that the data is consistent with the field format defined for the file. If any inconsistency is found, such as trying to store alpha information in a numeric field, the command is rejected. ADABAS itself does not have any facilities for validating the values of fields in any way, such as range checks. If ADAMINT is used these validations could be programmed into the interface module.

DMS 1100

DMS 1100 optionally allows data formats to be checked, and values to be validated. A CHECK clause may be specified at the record or field level to perform integrity checks. At the record level, the CHECK clause instructs DMS to verify that data loaded into the fields of the record is consistent with their definition. A database procedure, written by the DBA, may also be used to perform integrity checks.

When the CHECK clause is used at the field level a combination of checks can be performed. Data consistency checks can be requested, a procedure may be called, a range check can be performed on the data value or specific data values may be either allowed or disallowed.

IDMS

IDMS does not validate the format of the data fields within a record when they are STORED or MODIFYed. Redefinition of a record or a group field is supported so a programmer could move inconsistent data into a field. Database procedures could be written to perform integrity checks on the data.

IMS-DL/1

DL/1 does not validate the format of the data fields within a segment when they are Inserted or Replaced.

TOTAL

TOTAL does not validate the format of data being stored in the database. The system moves the specified information to or from the program without any checks or conversions.

MULTIPLE USER ACCESS

The techniques used by the five DBMSs for managing multiple user access are described in this section. It explains how the 'locking' mechanisms work and how deadly embraces are resolved.

A deadly embrace, or deadlock, can occur when two or more programs get into a situation where each program is waiting for one of the others to release a record that it needs to continue processing. The following sequence of events illustrates how two programs may become deadlocked.

Program 1   Reads and locks record A

Program 2   Reads and locks record B

Program 1   Requests record B
B is held elsewhere so the program waits for it to be released

Program 2   Requests record A
A is held elsewhere so the program waits for it to be released.

ADABAS

The multi-user version of ADABAS enables batch and on-line users to concurrently access and update the database. The concept of logical transaction is used to assure the logical integrity of the database. A logical transaction is the smallest number of database commands which must be executed by a user to maintain the data consistency of the database. Within a logical transaction, records from one or more database files may be read and held. This prevents other users from updating the same records and creating an inconsistent database. Held records are released when the user informs the system that the logical transaction is complete.

As a consequence of one user holding records other users may have to wait for an extended period until a record is released or a deadly embrace deadlock may develop. ADABAS handles this situation by limiting the time a command may wait to be processed. If the time expires the system assumes that a deadlock situation has developed. It then backs out the transaction which has been waiting the longest to its last 'End of Transaction' checkpoint. This procedure is repeated for each program until the deadlock is freed. Transactions which are backed out are informed of the system's action by means of a return code so that recovery action may be taken.

DMS 1100

DMS 1100 allows batch and on-line application programs to concurrently access and update the database. The logical integrity of the database is maintained by the use of 'locks' on resources which are being used by application programs. Resources which can be locked are database 'AREAs' (an AREA is an operating system file), database 'PAGEs' (a PAGE is a physical block on a file) and a RECORD.

An AREA lock is applied when a program, usually referred to as a run-unit, indicates that it wishes to update the AREA. No other run-unit may update the AREA while it is locked. The run-unit applying the lock may specify whether other retrieval run-units may run alongside the update or whether it is to have exclusive control of the AREA(s). AREA locks are not normally used by on-line run-units or when a high level of concurrency is required.

When concurrent updating of an AREA is permitted the PAGE and RECORD locking mechanisms protect the integrity of the database. When a run-unit causes a PAGE to be altered the PAGE is locked so that no other run-unit can alter it. Every PAGE altered is locked until the run-unit terminates the session (DEPART) or explicitly frees the resources it has locked.

A RECORD lock is applied to the record which is currently being accessed by a run-unit. A record may be held by more than one run-unit if they are all in retrieval mode. Run-units in update mode apply exclusive record locks since the record could be altered. By default only the record currently being accessed is locked, ie one per run-unit. However, a run-unit may explicitly lock the records accessed if required.

When DMS 1100 finds that a resource has already been locked by another run-unit it queues the request and suspends the requesting run-unit. When the resource becomes available the suspended run-unit is reactivated. It is possible that two (or more) run-units are each waiting for the other to free a resource thus causing a deadly embrace or deadlock. Deadly embrace situations are detected by means of a 'matrix' which is used to maintain details of all queued run-units. If a deadlock is detected the changes made to the database by one of the run-units are backed out and the run-unit is informed of this action by means of a return code so that it may either retry the transaction or terminate.

IDMS

The central version of IDMS permits batch and on-line users to concurrently access and update the database. The logical integrity of the database may be maintained in two ways. One method allows only one program at a time to update an identified subset of the database. This subset consists of one or more database AREAs. The program specifies whether other retrieval programs can run alongside the update or whether it is to have exclusive use of the subset of the database. This mode of protection is accomplished by means of 'AREA locks'. A flag maintained by IDMS is used to indicate whether the AREA is being updated. Area locks are even effective when there are multiple copies of IDMS attempting to update the database.

The second technique permits a number of programs to concurrently update the same subset of the database. A technique called 'record level locking' is used to maintain the logical integrity of the database. The records that a program is actively using are locked automatically in order to prevent a conflict between two or more programs updating the same record at the same time. Programs may also request the system to lock records which are not being actively used. This facility is used when it is necessary to update a number of records in order to maintain data integrity.

It is possible that a 'deadly embrace' may occur as a result of record locking. IDMS has two mechanisms for detecting this situation. The locking algorithm can detect simple deadlock situations. It is also possible to specify the maximum time that a program may wait for a record to be freed. When a deadlock condition is detected the program causing the deadlock or the program which has exceeded the time limit is backed out to the last checkpoint. Programs which are backed out in this way are informed of the system's action by means of a return code so that they can either retry the transaction or terminate gracefully.

ICL implementations use 'PAGE locks' instead of 'RECORD locks'. Two different techniques are sometimes employed. In the first all pages accessed, irrespective of whether they are updated, are locked. If the page is only to be read other applications may also read it, but they may not update it. If the page is read in update mode no other application may access it. Pages are only unlocked when the application indicates that an update sequence has completed.

The second technique uses two types of page lock: a *retrieve lock* and an *update lock*. A page may be retrieve locked by more than one application. When a page is updated it is changed to an update lock. A page with an update lock cannot be accessed by other applications. However an update lock can only be applied when no other application has retrieve locked the page.

IMS-DL/1

A DL/1 database may be concurrently accessed and updated by a number of users. 'Data Sharing' allows multiple copies of DL/1 to access the same database. Sharing at the 'Database' level allows one copy to update while other copies are only permitted retrieval access. 'Block' level sharing (IMS MVS only) enables copies which support on-line systems to update concurrently. The operating system file sharing options may also be used to control concurrent access.

When one copy of DL/1 is being shared by a number of users one of two techniques is used to maintain the integrity of the data. Systems with limited storage and processing capacity would use 'Intent Scheduling'. Systems requiring a greater degree of concurrency normally use 'Program Isolation'.

Intent Scheduling causes a task to be scheduled according to the way in which it wishes to access the data. A task's intent is indicated in a control block known as the Program Specification Block (PSB) which specifies which parts of the database the task may access. If one task is accessing a segment type with update intent then a second task wishing to access the same segment type with update intent has to wait until the first task terminates and releases the segment type. Possible intent conflicts are identified at initialisation time so deadlocks cannot occur. A task 'locks' all the segment types it may wish to update at initialisation time.

Program Isolation operates at the segment occurrence level. It consists of two functional areas; contention management and deadlock avoidance. Contention management allows a number of tasks to concurrently update segments of the same type provided that each task is accessing mutually exclusive occurrences of the segment type. Once a task has accessed a given segment with update intent no other task may access that segment (not even read only tasks) until the task reaches a synchronization point or completes.

It is possible that deadly embrace situations may develop when segment occurrence locking is used. This happens when two or more tasks are waiting for resources held by other tasks which are also waiting. Deadlock avoidance recognises such situations and terminates a task in an attempt to resolve that deadlock. On-line tasks are terminated in preference to batch tasks. If the tasks are of the same type, ie batch or on-line, the one holding the fewest resources is terminated. The terminated task is dynamically backed out and automatically restarted.

TOTAL

A TOTAL database may be concurrently accessed and updated by a number of users. When a number of copies of TOTAL are running concurrently using the same database the logical integrity of the data is preserved by the use of file locks. Once one copy of the software has opened part of the database for update no other copy is permitted to open the same part of the database for update until the first copy indicates that it has finished updating.

This locking mechanism is implemented by setting a flag on each database file that is open for update. If a program fails during an update run the flag will not be reset. Programs will not be able to update the potentially corrupted part of the database until the Data Base Administrator has investigated the failure and recovered the database. A utility can be used to reset the lock if it is known that the database has not been corrupted.

The central version of TOTAL allows multiple batch or on-line users to concurrently access and update the database. Database records may be read and held by an application program. Other users may access a held record but they cannot update it. Application programs must be designed to maintain the data consistency of the database by ensuring that all the records to be updated, and records which are to be accessed for information, which must not be altered by another application during the update, are held for the duration of the update sequence.

A held record is released when the program holding it updates the record. All the records held by a program are released when the program closes the database or terminates. A program may also be forced to release a held record by the deadlock resolution algorithm.

As a result of one program holding records, another program may have to wait for the record to be released so a deadly embrace deadlock may develop. TOTAL handles this situation by informing the requesting program that the record is currently held by another user. The program may be designed to repeatedly retry the request until the required record has been released by the other user. This will cater for the situation where the record was simply 'busy' when it was first requested but the programs would loop forever if a deadly embrace deadlock has developed. In order to prevent this happening TOTAL allows a record to be 'stolen' from the program that has locked it if another user requests the record more than a specified number of times. The program which has the record stolen from it, and assumed to be the cause of the deadlock, is informed of the system's action through a response code.

When TOTAL is supporting teleprocessing system users the record holding mechanism works differently. If the database is to be updated all records accessed are held until the transaction indicates that the update is complete (by signing off explicitly free held resources or COMITing the changes already made). If a deadly embrace occurs, TOTAL returns a status code to the program so transactions need to be programmed to free the resources they are holding and retry the transaction.

4 Language Interfaces

The objectives of this chapter are to:

— categorise the language interfaces available and explain why they are important;

and for each of the five DBMSs to:

— describe how the DBMS interfaces with application programs;

— consider the Data Definition facilities;

— describe the Data Manipulation Language.

INTRODUCTION

A DBMS must provide facilities for defining and accessing a database. Such facilities are made available by various language interfaces. These languages may take the form of a high-level language or, alternatively, they may be parametric.

Two major categories of language interface with a DBMS may be identified: Data Manipulation Languages (DML) and Data Definition (or Description) Languages (DDL). Both language categories may be subdivided.

A user wishing to access, update or add data to the database communicates with it through a language interface which allows the data to be manipulated, hence the term Data Manipulation. Three types of Data Manipulation facilities can be listed:

— *Host Language DML*. This is the language used by application programmers to transfer data between the database and application programs. The application programs are written in host languages, such as COBOL, PL/1 and FORTRAN, which provide the facilities for printing or performing arithmetic on the data. When the term DML is used in this book it refers to this form of data manipulation facility.

— *Report Writers.* A report writer is a software package which provides facilities for selecting, formatting and printing data from the database. Generally, non-database files may also be accessed. A report writer runs in a batch environment and is driven by a control language specific to the package. Report writers enable reports to be produced much more quickly and easily than conventional programming languages (COBOL, etc).

— *Query/Update Languages.* A query language provides on-line facilities for selecting, formatting and printing/displaying data from the database. Query languages provide real-time responses to the user's requests for data. A number of 'query' languages permit update.

Some systems have what are sometimes known as Self Contained Languages. These provide the same facilities as Report Writers and Query Languages.

This book only discusses the host language DML facilities in more detail. The vendors of all the five DBMSs described do market both a Report Writer and a Query System.

In order to establish a database on a computer it is necessary to define its structure. The data-items or fields of data, the way in which these fields are combined to form groups or records and the relationships between different record types need to be defined. A language used for describing the data in this way is called a Data Definition Language or a Data Description Language (DDL).

Some DBMSs rely on one DDL to describe the logical and physical organisation of the data. Others subdivide the description of the data into three parts:

— *The global logical view of the data.* This describes the data and the relationships between the data for the whole database, hence the term global view. The data is described in purely logical terms. No assumptions are made about the physical organisation of the data.

The technical term for such a description is a schema. A schema is defined as a map of the overall logical structure of the database.

— *Local views of the data.* A local view describes the view of the database which a user or programmer is permitted to see. Such a view is a subset of the global view. There may be a mapping between the global and local views so the data seen by the user may have a different description to that in the global description. Since the local view is a subset of the global view it is generally called a subschema. Usually there will be a number of subschemas associated with a database describing different views of the data for various groups of users.

— *Physical organisation of the data.* The physical organisation defines the way in which the data in the global view is mapped onto physical storage within the computer. Such a description is called a Device Media Control or Service Description specification.

The three views described above represent the ideal way of describing the data. In practice the distinction between the global, local and physical views of the data is not so clear cut.

The interfaces between the outside world, which includes the data processing department, and a DBMS are very important. If a DBMS is being selected these interfaces should be studied in detail. They determine:

— The ease, or otherwise, with which data may be defined and manipulated. Consideration should be given to the training time required to become competent in their use. This is especially important for the DML as the turnover of programmers can result in high recurrent training costs.

— The complexity of the interface and the likelihood of errors being made. The level of skill required to use the system must be considered. For example does a programmer have to fully understand the multi-user facilities or is sharing dealt with automatically? The consequences of an error also need to be considered as well as the diagnostic facilities of the DBMS.

— The manipulation capabilities of the software. The DML commands provided determine the ways in which the data may be accessed. A restricted set of commands may increase the complexity of application programs if it is necessary to program around their shortcomings.

Later in this chapter the DDL and the DML facilities of the five DBMSs are described. The aim is to give the reader a general impression of the facilities available. The syntax of the languages is not included. If the reader requires more detailed information the appropriate vendors' reference manuals should be consulted.

DBMS INTERFACE TO APPLICATION PROGRAMS

This section briefly describes the type of interface between application programs and the DBMS for each of the five DBMSs. There are two types of interface. First, there is the type where the programmer codes 'CALL' statements to the DBMS. The second type allows the programmer to use commands which are extensions of the host programming language.

The programmer may view the DBMS as a service routine which is called to perform specific services. It is like calling sophisticated read/write subroutines or issuing COBOL READ/WRITE statements. A response code (sometimes called a return code or status code) is used to inform the program whether or not the service was successfully completed. Its value indicates the reason why a request could not be satisfied. The response code is either one of the CALL parameters or alternatively one of the fields contained in a control block held in the program's working storage.

ADABAS

ADABAS can be used with either a high-level or a low-level data manipulation language interface. Both rely on the host language 'CALL' facilities and programmer coded parameter lists to pass control and information to and from the database software. Programs can be written in COBOL, PL/1, FORTRAN or ASSEMBLER.

The high-level DML enables the programmer to 'CALL' an interface module, specifying at most three parameters, which accesses and manipulates a subset of the database. The interface module is generated by the Data Base Administrator, using software called ADAMINT, to present the application program with a simplified view of the data. This functional interface simplifies application programming and allows the DBA to control the database.

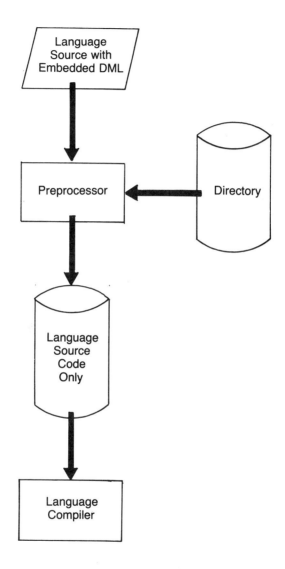

Figure 15   DMS 1100 and IDMS Preprocessor

The low-level DML allows the program to 'CALL' ADABAS directly. A control block and up to five separate buffer areas, depending on the command, must be passed as parameters. Most new users avoid this low-level DML in order to simplify application programming.

DMS 1100

Application programs communicate with DMS 1100 through a high-level Data Manipulation Language (DML). The DML consists of meaningful verbs and condition statements which are logical extensions of the host programming language. A preprocessor is used to convert the DML statements into host language 'CALL' requests (Figure 15). Preprocessors are available for COBOL, PL/1 and FORTRAN.

The preprocessor copies the required record data descriptions into the program from a library. This automatically ensures that the program's description of the data corresponds with that defined in the subschema. It also forces programs to use the defined names for addressing database components.

IDMS

Application programs use a high-level Data Manipulation Language (DML) to interface with IDMS. The programmer codes meaningful DML verbs and condition statements which are logical extensions of the host language. An IDMS preprocessor (or precompiler) is used to convert the DML statements into host language 'CALL' requests (Figure 15). Preprocessors are available for COBOL, PL/1, FORTRAN and ASSEMBLER.

The preprocessor copies the required data descriptions into the program from the Directory. This automatically ensures that the program's description of the data corresponds with that defined in the schema or subschema. It also ensures that all database programs use a standard set of names for addressing database components. Non-database record descriptions and codes can be manually catalogued to the Directory and selectively copied into a program by the preprocessor.

IMS-DL/1

Application programs interface to the database through DL/1's Data Manipulation Language (DML) which relies on the host language

'CALL' facilities. Programs issue calls to DL/1 with a function code and an associated list of parameters. Programs may be written in COBOL, PL/1, ASSEMBLER, and DOS-RPG.

TOTAL

Application programs interface with the database through TOTAL's Data Manipulation Language (DML) which relies on the host language 'CALL' facilities and programmer coded parameter lists to pass control and information to and from the database software. Programs can be written in COBOL, PL/1, FORTRAN, RPG or ASSEMBLER.

DATA DEFINITION LANGUAGES

This section describes the overall structure of the Data Definition facilities for each of the five DBMSs. As will be seen some systems rely on the use of utilities to define the data. Others have from one to three special languages for describing various aspects of the data.

ADABAS

The components of an ADABAS database are defined by the use of a number of utility functions. The basic components are files, records, fields, descriptor keys and possibly coupling relationships.

An ADABAS file is defined by a utility which catalogues its record format into the Associator and describes the characteristics of each field of the record. The physical space for the file is defined and allocated from Data Storage when the file is loaded. A utility is provided which produces a database status report. This report documents the record formats and gives details of any coupling relationships.

The ADABAS DDL comprises the control statements used to drive the utilities which define record formats, descriptors, etc. These control statements have a simple positional and keyword parameter format.

DMS 1100

There are two levels of data definition in DMS 1100. The SCHEMA level is defined with the Schema Data Description Language (DDL). The SUBSCHEMA level is defined using the Subschema Data Description Language (SDDL).

The DDL consists of an IDENTIFICATION DIVISION and a DATA DIVISION. The IDENTIFICATION DIVISION provides the schema with a name and optional control locks. The DATA DIVISION consists of up to five sections:

DATA NAME SECTION
This optional section defines fields referenced in the DDL which are not area, record type, field or set identifiers.

AREA SECTION
All the AREAs which comprise the database are defined. Size, space management, logging and access control information is specified for each AREA.

RECORD SECTION
All the Records in the database are defined. The location mode, area or areas in which it may be stored, access control information, record layout, field size, field format and checking criteria for each record are specified.

SET SECTION
SET relationships in the database are defined. Set mode, set order, set selection and access control information is specified for each set.

TABLE SECTION
This optional section is used when a field defined in a record is 'encoded' using a table.

The subschema description consists of an IDENTIFICATION DIVISION and a DATA DIVISION. The IDENTIFICATION DIVISION names the subschema and identifies which language the programs that will use it are coded in. The DATA DIVISION consists of the same five sections used to define the schema.

IDMS

IDMS uses three levels of data definition. These are the Schema Data Description Language, the Device Media Control Language (or Service Description Language) and the Subschema Data Description Language.

The schema data definition comprises the following descriptive sections:

SCHEMA DESCRIPTION
This section provides the schema with a name and allows other documentary entries to be made.

FILE DESCRIPTION
Names the physical files used to hold the database and journal (log) file.

AREA DESCRIPTION
Describes the way in which the database is to be divided into Areas and how these Areas are to be mapped onto the physical files.

RECORD DESCRIPTION
All the record types are defined. The location mode, Areas where they are to be stored and a description of the record layout, field sizes and formats are specified for each record.

SET DESCRIPTION
This section describes the set relationships between pairs of record types. The set order, set linkage options and set membership options are specified for each set.

INDEX DESCRIPTION
In some implementations this section is used to specify the indexes to be used.

The DMCL consists of a DEVICE-MEDIA DESCRIPTION or SERVICE DESCRIPTION which gives the Device Media Control Block a name and allows other documentary entries to be made. This is followed by these SECTION entries:

BUFFER SECTION
This specifies the buffering requirements such as the number of buffers to be used.

AREA SECTION
Identifies the Areas that may be accessed by the user of the DMCB. It is also possible to specify space management information for each area.

LOCK SECTION
In some implementations this section specifies the number of entries in the page locking table, the deadlock time out interval and the maximum number of threads to be supported.

FILE SECTION
Provided in some implementations to allow the page sizes specified
in the schema to be overridden.

JOURNAL SECTION
This describes the file or files to be used as journals.

The subschema data description is considered to be a part of the host
programming language. The IDMS subschema language is based on the
COBOL programming language. Two DIVISIONs are coded to define a
subschema. The SUBSCHEMA IDENTIFICATION DIVISION names
the subschema, the DMCB to be used with it and also allows other
documentary entries to be made. The SUBSCHEMA DATA DIVISION
contains three SECTIONS:

AREA SECTION
Names the Areas which the subschema may access together with the
Area Privacy Locks.

RECORD SECTION
Identifies the Records which the subschema may access and defines
the Record Privacy Locks. Record descriptions may be either copied
in from the directory or, alternatively, a subset of the record may be
defined.

SET SECTION
Identifies the relationships which may be used and specifies the Set
Privacy Locks.

The schema, DMCB and subschema information is stored in the Directory. A utility is provided which reports on its contents. Information can
be requested for all or selected schemas, subschemas, DMCBs, files,
areas, records and sets. Comments may be added to the Record field
descriptions in the schema data definition which are printed on the
Record Reports.

IMS-DL/1

There are two levels of data definition in DL/1. The Data Base Definitions (DBD) define the logical and physical structure of the data. The
Program Specification Block (PSB) defines the programmer's local view
of the database.

The DBD is specified using the following macros. A number of FIELD macros would normally follow a SEGM macro. All the segments in the hierarchy are defined by repeated use of the SEGM and FIELD macros.

DBD
Defines the type of DBD as physical, logical or index. A physical DBD defines the access method to be used for a physical database (file or data set). A logical DBD defines a logical structure composed of segments from physical databases (files). An index DBD is used to define a HIDAM index and secondary indexes.

DATASET
For a physical DBD, this defines the physical characteristics of the dataset or file.

SEGM
Defines a segment and its parent(s). Pointer requirements and insertion rules are also specified.

FIELD
Names the fields contained in the segment. One field may be defined as a sequence field (Key).

LCHILD
Defines a segment as a Logical Child. It is also used to define the Index record for HIDAM, and the Index Pointer Segments used for secondary indexes.

XDFLD
Only used when an Index DBD is defined. It specifies how the index key is constructed from up to five other fields.

DBDGEN
Marks the end of the DBD generation, macros.

The PSB is specified using the following macros. A number of PCBs may be specified. For each PCB the SENSEG macros identify the segments which may be referenced. Each SENSEG macro may be followed by a list of the fields within the segment that the program may access.

PCB
Identifies the DBD (physical or logical) that defines the database record to be accessed. The processing options, ie access authorisation, are defined. An index may also be specified.

SENSEG
Names the segments to which the program is sensitive. Only segments that are part of hierarchical access paths which the program
needs to access need to be specified. (A hierarchical access path
consists of a segment type from each level of the hierarchy down to
the segment type to which access is required.) SENSEG statements
enable a local program view of a database record and access rights to
be specified.

SENFLD
Identifies the fields (and their order) to which the program is sensitive.

PSBGEN
Names the PSB and the host language to which it must interface.

TOTAL

The data in a TOTAL database is represented by one or more Data Base
Definition Modules (DBMODs). The DBMODs are specified with
TOTAL's Data Base Definition Languages (DBDL).

The DBDL is used to specify the details of all the files which are needed
for the DBMOD's local view of the database. The physical and logical
structure of each file is defined. This includes the buffer requirements;
the file size; the level, name and length of each field; and the linkage
paths.

The Master Data Set statements are used to define the unique control
key. Variable Entry Data Set statements allow coded, or redefined,
records to be specified and loading conditions to be defined.

DATA MANIPULATION LANGUAGES

The host language DMLs for the five DBMSs are described in this
section. The aim is to describe, in general terms, the manipulation
facilities provided. In order to illustrate the power of the DML the main
commands are briefly described. The commands are grouped into three
categories, namely control, retrieval and modification statements.

When a programmer writes a program which accesses a database
containing numerous occurrences of many different record types it is
important to know which records are currently in use. The DBMS main-

tains the current coordinates of a program within the data structure by means of 'currency' or 'positioning' indicators. Usually, the programmer does not need to be concerned with these in detail but an understanding of them is required. Currency indicators are usually the internal addresses of the records being used.

ADABAS

ADABAS may be used with any programming language which supports a 'CALL' statement, such as COBOL, PL/1, FORTRAN and ASSEM-BLER. Since the DML is implemented through the use of standard host language facilities there is no need to use a preprocessor. Database programs are compiled and link edited like non-database programs. Two levels of DML are supported, a High-Level DML and a Low-Level DML.

When the High-Level DML is used the programmer CALLs a user defined entry point in an Interface Module. The Interface Module consists of one or more Access Modules which access the database using low-level DML commands. Each Access Module defines a logical 'view' of the data which is needed by the program. 'ADAMINT' macros are used to generate these modules.

The use of the interface module makes it possible to present the program with logical records which are tailored to its needs. A logical record can be specified as one or more fields arranged in any desired order and with any format and length. It is also possible to build a logical record containing information from a number of ADABAS files. There are three categories of ADAMINT functions: Data Selection and Retrieval; Data Modification; and Control functions. These functions are briefly described below. The programmer requests a given function by calling a user named entry point to the access module.

Data Selection and Retrieval functions:

FINDSET
Finds the records which satisfy a search argument. The number of records found is returned in a parameter.

READSET
Reads data from a record found by a previous FINDSET into the program's data-area. All the records found can be read by repeated use of this call.

LOKATE
Prepare to start reading from the record with a value equal to or greater than that specified in one of the parameters.

SEQREAD
Reads sequentially from the point defined by a previous LOKATE. Repeated use of this call will cause records to be returned sequentially.

REREAD
The previously read record is reread. This call may only be used after READSET or SEQREAD.

LOKVAL
This is used with READVAL to read the descriptor values in the Associator. The index to the data is read, not the data records. It prepares to start reading the descriptor values equal to or greater than that specified in one of the parameters.

READVAL
The value of the descriptor is read into the program's data-area and the number of records containing this value is returned in one of the parameters. Repeated use of this call causes the descriptor to read sequentially.

Data Modification functions:

UPDATER
This updates the logical record contained in the program's data-area. The DBA determines the record format when the Access Module is generated. The Access Module will then update the database at the field level, by updating each field included in the logical record. This call is only valid after a SEQREAD, READSET and REREAD.

ADDNEW
The logical record contained in the program's data-area is added to the database. The Access Module determines the format of the logical record. When the corresponding database record is stored fields not included in the logical record are set to null values.

DELETER
This deletes a single record from a file. This call can only be used after a SEQREAD, READSET or REREAD. The previously read record is deleted.

RELEASE

This call is used if the Access Module was generated to 'HOLD' a record which has been read because it may be updated or deleted. The update or deletion will normally release the HOLD. If it is decided that the record should not be updated or deleted this call is used to release the HOLD.

Control functions:

SIGNON

This starts the database session. A run-mode parameter defines whether this is a test run or not, and the user's password.

SIGNOFF

This terminates the database session.

MINTET

This call informs the system that a logical update transaction has been completed. Any records which have been held are released. User data may be logged which can be used to assist in restart after a failure.

MINTBT

The current logical transaction is backed out.

MINTRE

The data stored by the last MINTET call is read. This data may also be read by the SIGNON call.

CHEKPNT

This causes a checkpoint to be taken.

SNAPINT

This dumps the communications areas in the Access Module.

RCANAL

The response code is analysed and converted into a cause-code and an explanatory message.

When the low-level DML is used, the programmer CALLs ADABAS directly. The programmer must provide a control block and up to five buffer areas, depending upon the command, for each call. A command code and other control information is placed into the control block in order to request ADABAS services.

The five buffers are known as Control Buffers. The SEARCH BUF-FER contains a logical search argument which may contain logical operators. The search argument does not contain any actual values, the programmer loads these into a VALUE BUFFER. A search command results in a list of the ISNs of the records satisfying the search argument being placed into an ISN BUFFER. If the number of records found exceeds the capacity of the ISN BUFFER the programmer must load the buffer with batches of ISNs by placing additional control information into the control block.

A FORMAT BUFFER is used to identify the fields which are required. The programmer may also specify what length and data format the information is to be presented in. This allows the format of the logical record used within the program to be defined. The logical record is read into, or written from a RECORD BUFFER.

A large number of data selection/retrieval, data modification and control codes are provided.

DMS 1100

The DMS 1100 Data Manipulation Language is based on the CODASYL recommendations. It is a high-level interface with data manipulation commands which are an extension of the host language. The program source code must be preprocessed to convert the DML commands into host language CALLs and copy in record descriptions before it can be compiled. Preprocessors are available for COBOL, PL/1 and FORTRAN.

The DML consists of declarative statements and executable com-mands. For COBOL the declarative statements are placed in the DATA DIVISION in a new section, following the FILE SECTION, called the SUBSCHEMA SECTION. This section is used to identify the subschema to be invoked and the error handling procedures.

The preprocessor uses the information in the SUBSCHEMA SEC-TION to generate entries in the WORKING STORAGE SECTION and/or the COMMON STORAGE SECTION. These entries include a communications block which is used to interface to the Data Manage-ment Routine (DMR) and the descriptions of the records to be used.

The executable DML commands can be grouped into three categories:

control, retrieval and modification commands. Each command is briefly described below.

Control statements:

IMPART
The run-unit indicates that it wishes to use the database.

OPEN
This identifies the AREAs to be used and the mode (Update, Retrieval, etc) in which they are to be accessed. Either all the AREAs specified in a subschema can be opened or a named subset.

CLOSE
Either all the AREAs, or the AREAs named in the command, are closed.

DEPART
This indicates that the run-unit has finished using the database. The run-unit may optionally request the system to rollback (restore) any changes it has made to the database.

KEEP
This allows a run-unit to hold the record most recently accessed, even though the record has not been altered in any way. Pages containing records which are altered are automatically locked.

FREE
Locked resources are released and the log information maintained for automatic rollback (the Quick-Before Looks which are discussed in the section on Recovery and Restart) is deleted. The changes already made to the database will not be automatically backed out if the run-unit subsequently fails.

LOG
This allows a run-unit to place user information onto the audit trail log. Information required to restart the run-unit could be logged.

MOVE
This enables a run-unit to save control information for later use in the same run.

IF
This tests whether a set is empty or whether a record is a member of a set.

Retrieval statements:

FIND
The record identified by the command parameters is located by the system but is not moved into the program's record area.

GET
A record which has previously been located by a FIND command is moved into the program's record area.

FETCH
This is the equivalent of a FIND immediately followed by a GET.

ACQUIRE
This retrieves database keys for the current array set.

Modification statements:

STORE
A new record is added to the database from the run-unit's record area.

MODIFY
An updated record is written back to the database from the run-unit's record area.

DELETE
This deletes one or more records from the database. If the record to be deleted is an owner of other records the deletion may either be suppressed or they may also be deleted. Either automatic or manual and automatic members can be deleted with their owner.

INSERT
This allows a record to be linked into a set.

REMOVE
This enables a record to be de-linked from a set.

Programmers navigate round the database using the DML commands. The current position in the database is recorded by CURRENCY indicators. There are four types of currency indicators – Run-Unit, Record Type, Set Type and Area Type. These are described below:

Run-Unit
The address of the record occurrence most recently accessed.

Record Type

For each record type: the address of the most recently accessed record of that type.

Set

For each set: the address of the most recently accessed record in the set (it could be a member or an owner).

Area

For each area: the address of the most recently accessed record in the area.

These currency indicators change as the programmer navigates through the database. The various DML commands cause currency to change in different but common sense ways. Currency changes resulting from the execution of a particular DML command can optionally be suppressed.

Programmers do not need to know how the data is physically structured but they do need to be familiar with the logical structure of the part of the database they are using. If the database is to be concurrently updated, programmers must appreciate the possibility of creating data inconsistency in the special situation when records are not updated on their first access if records are not held (KEEP command) when necessary. They must also be aware that they can delay other users if resources are held for longer than necessary.

IDMS

The IDMS Data Manipulation Language is also based on the CODASYL recommendations. Its data manipulation commands are extensions of the host language. Program source code is preprocessed to convert the DML commands into host language CALLs before it is compiled. Preprocessors are available for COBOL, PL/1, FORTRAN and ASSEMBLER.

The DML consists of declarative statements and executable commands. The declarative statements for COBOL are placed in the DATA DIVISION, in an additional section, following the FILE SECTION, called the SCHEMA SECTION. This section is used to define which subschema is to be invoked and which records are to be accessed.

The preprocessor uses the information in the SCHEMA SECTION to generate entries in the WORKING STORAGE SECTION and/or the

LINKAGE SECTION. A block is copied into working storage for communication between the program and IDMS.

The DML commands can be grouped into four categories: control, retrieval, modification and save commands. A brief description of each command type is given below.

Control statements:

BIND
The program names the subschema to be used and optionally identifies which records in the subschema will actually be used.

READY
This identifies the AREAs which are to be used and their mode of use. All the AREAs referenced in the subschema can be 'readied' or a named subset. This command is similar to a conventional file OPEN.

FINISH
This indicates that the program has finished accessing the database.

COMMIT
A checkpoint is taken. If an error occurs the automatic rollback facility will rollback the program to the most recent COMMIT checkpoint.

ROLLBACK
The program requests IDMS to back out any changes made to the database since the program started or the most recent checkpoint if a COMMIT command has previously been used.

KEEP
This allows a program to hold a record so that no other program may update or possibly access it.

Retrieval Statements:

FIND
The record identified by the FIND command is located by IDMS but it is not moved into the record area in the program.

GET
A record which has previously been found (FIND statement) is moved into the program's record area.

OBTAIN
This is equivalent to a FIND followed by a GET.

Modification Statements:

STORE
A new record is added to the database.

MODIFY
An updated record is rewritten to the database from the program's record area.

CONNECT
A record may be added into a set which was declared with a set membership option of 'OPTIONAL'.

DISCONNECT
A record may be removed from a set which was declared with a set membership option of 'OPTIONAL'.

ERASE
Deletes one or more records from the database.

Save Statement:

ACCEPT
The program may save access control information for use later in the run. Usage statistics may also be obtained using this command.

The program navigates around the database using the DML commands. The current co-ordinates in the database are recorded by CURRENCY indicators. In common with other CODASYL systems there are four types of currency indicator – Run-Unit, Record Type, Set and Area.

Run-Unit
The address of the record occurrence most recently accessed.

Record Type
For each record type, the address of the most recently accessed record of that type.

Set
For each set, the address of the most recently accessed record in the set. (It could be a member of the set or its owner.)

Area

For each area, the address of the most recently accessed record in the area.

As the programmer navigates through the database using the DML commands the currency indicator will change to indicate the current state of processing. The DML commands change the currency indicators in various but common sense ways.

The programmer does not need to be aware of the physical storage structure of the database. Programmers must, however, be familiar with the logical structure of the part of the database in use. If the database is being updated in a multi-user mode the programmer needs to be aware of the possibility of creating data inconsistency if records which are to be updated are not locked properly. An appreciation of the need to free locked records as soon as possible in order to avoid delaying other users is also required.

IMS-DL/1

DL/1 can be used by programs written in COBOL, PL/1, ASSEMBLER and DOS-RPG. The DML is implemented through the use of the host language CALL facilities. Database programs are therefore compiled and link edited in the same way as non-database programs; there is no preprocessor step.

A DL/1 host language dependent subroutine is called by the programmer. The programmer sets up a list of parameters which specify the database service required. The services available are documented in order to illustrate the capabilities of the DML. There are three types of facilities: retrieval, update and system service functions.

A DL/1 request consists of a function code, a PCB-name, I/O Area and an optional SSA list. The PCB-name identifies the Program Control Block within the Program Specification Block which defines the data structure to be accessed. The I/O Area identifies the area in the application program into which data is read or from which data is written. One Segment Search Argument (SSA) may be provided for each segment type accessed in a hierarchical path. Each SSA identifies the segment selection criteria. The SSA is discussed more fully later in this section.

Retrieval Functions:

GET UNIQUE AND GET HOLD UNIQUE
DL/1 retrieves the segment(s) identified by the SSA list. If no SSA list is provided the system positions itself at the first occurrence of the root segment type. The main use of this function is to position the program at the required database record.

The hold function informs the system that the retrieved segment(s) may be updated. Other segments in the path are not held. The hold is automatically released by the next DL/1 call against the same PCB.

GET NEXT AND GET HOLD NEXT
Once a position within the database has been established this function may be used to retrieve segments in hierarchical sequence (ie proceeding from top to bottom, and left to right) within a structure and forward through the database. An SSA list may be used to skip forward to a selected segment. The next or SSA identified segment(s) is transferred to the program's data area.

The hold function informs the system that the segment retrieved may be updated. The next DL/1 call against the same PCB releases the hold.

Status codes in the PCB inform the programmer of changes in the level of the hierarchy being processed.

GET NEXT WITHIN PARENT AND GET HOLD NEXT WITHIN PARENT
This function allows segments which are dependents of a previously identified parent to be retrieved in hierarchical sequence. The parent is the segment retrieved by a previous Get Next or Get Unique call. An SSA list may be used to selectively retrieve this parent's dependent segments.

The hold function is used when the retrieved segment may be updated. The hold is released by the next DL/1 call against the same PCB.

Status codes in the PCB inform the programmer of changes in the level of the hierarchy being processed.

Update Functions:

INSERT
The insert function is used to add a new segment, which is built in the

program's I/O Area, to the database. At least one SSA must be specified to identify the type of the segment being inserted. If only one SSA is specified the program must have been positioned to the new segment's parent. Alternatively, the point of insertion may be specified through an SSA list.

A segment with a sequence field (Key) is inserted into its parent's family of this segment type so as to maintain an ascending key sequence; duplicates are placed following existing segments with the same Key.

If no sequence field (Key) is defined for the segment type the insertion rules (FIRST, LAST, HERE) specified in the DBD are used to determine the point of insertion.

DELETE
The delete function is used to delete a segment and any dependent segments it may have. A delete function must follow the Get Hold command which retrieved the segment being deleted. No SSA list is required since the position of the segment is established by the preceding Get Hold function.

REPLACE
The replace function is used to rewrite a modified segment. A Get Hold command must be used to read the segment. No SSA list is required since the position of the segment is established by the preceding Get Hold function.

If the segment has a sequence field (Key) this must not be modified. The system will detect an attempt to change it.

System Service Functions:

STATISTICS
This function gives the program access to DL/1 system statistics. A call parameter specifies which statistics are to be returned to the program's I/O Area.

LOG
This function enables an application program to write information to the DL/1 log.

ROLL (IMS)
The system rolls back the requesting transaction.

CHECKPOINT

This function forces DL/1 to rewrite all its modified buffers back to the database. A checkpoint record is written to the DL/1 log.

THE SEGMENT SEARCH ARGUMENT

The SSA consists of a segment name, an optional command code and an optional qualification statement. The segment type name is used to define an access path to the data structure. An access path is defined by a list of SSAs each identifying one segment type from successive levels of the hierarchy. If an SSA is omitted the first segment type is assumed by default; if a lower level SSA is specified the previous level is implicitly uniquely defined.

The optional qualification statement allows a logical test to be performed on the named field within the segment type occurrences. An example is provided in Figure 16. Only segments satisfying the test are considered in a Get function. IMS allows a number of qualification statements to be chained together by 'AND' or 'OR' to form a Boolean equation.

The optional command codes extend the facilities of the functional calls. For example a Path Call may be specified. A Get function reads all or selected segments of an access path. An Insert function writes all of the segments of the access path defined by the SSA list. If a replace function follows a Path Call all of the segments read will, by default, be rewritten. If a segment has not been modified a code can be used to suppress the rewrite. A command code also allows segments retrieved by a call to be locked so that no other user can retrieve them. Segments locked in this way are released when the program releases them or completes.

The programmer must ensure that the 'position' (cf currency) within the database is established, using a Get Unique function, before attempting to use other functions. A knowledge of how the position changes after DL/1 calls is also required. Two modes of positioning are available, Single and Multiple. Single positioning causes DL/1 to maintain only one position for a PCB. Multiple positioning allows position information to be maintained for each hierarchical path within the data structure. The result of a sequence of DL/1 calls will be different for each mode so the programmer must be aware of the positioning specified for each PCB.

Programmers do not need to know how the data is physically structured but they do need to be familiar with the logical structure that their

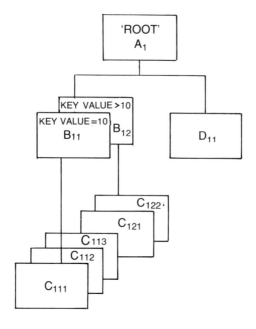

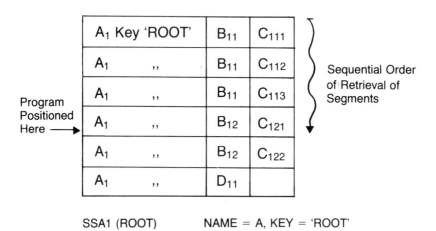

Figure 16   DL/1 Segment Search Argument

program is sensitive to, ie their local view. If the database is to be concurrently updated the programmer must appreciate the possibility of retrieval inconsistencies if segments are not held when necessary. For example a segment could be retrieved (but not held) early in the program, updated by another user and then retrieved with hold for update.

Programmers should also be aware that they can delay other users if resources are held unnecessarily.

TOTAL

TOTAL may be used with any programming language that supports a 'CALL' statement such as COBOL, PL/1, FORTRAN and ASSEMBLER. The system does not have a symbolic DML and therefore does not have a preprocessor. Database programs are compiled and link edited in the same way as non-database programs.

A subroutine, called 'DATBAS', is called with a list of parameters which are set up by the programmer. These parameters are used to specify what database services are required. The service functions available are documented below in order to demonstrate the power of the DML. These fall into three categories, Retrieval, Modification and Control functions.

Retrieval functions:

FINDX – Find
A specified data set is searched for records which satisfy the logical equation set up in one of the parameters. A parameter allows the programmer to specify whether the search should be serial and where the serial scan should start or whether a named linkpath should be scanned.

RDNXT – Read Next
The named data set is read and the items named in a data-list are placed in the program's data-area. The file can be read either serially from a specified point or by following a linkpath in a Variable Entry Data Set.

READD – Read Direct
If the internal number (ie its relative record address in direct access storage) of a record is known it may be read by using this command. A valid linkage path and control key must be specified.

READM – Read Master
The required elements contained in the master record identified by its control key are placed in the program's data-area.

READR – Read Reverse
A specified linkage path is read backwards. The read may be started from the end of a linkpath or from a specified record within it.

READV – Read Variable
A specified linkage path is read forward. The read may be started from the start of a linkpath or from a specified record within it.

RQLOC – Request Location
The control key is hashed to generate the internal reference number of the record. This reference number is placed in the program's data-area.

Modification functions:

ADD-M – Add Master
A new record containing the elements specified in a data-list is added to the data set. The control key is hashed to determine its storage location. A check is made for duplicate keys.

ADDVA – Add Variable After
A new record is added to a specified linkpath after the one that is identified by one of the parameters. The record is automatically added to the end of any other linkpaths that it may participate in.

ADDVB – Add Variable Before
A new record is added to a specified linkpath before the one that is identified by one of the parameters. The record is automatically added to the end of any other linkpaths that it may participate in.

ADDVC – Add Variable Continue
A new record is added at the end of all the linkage paths defined that it participates in.

ADDVR – Add Variable Replace
The specified record is logically relinked. Control field values may have changed so TOTAL may need to link the record into different occurrences of the linkpath.

DEL-M – Delete Master
A Master record identified by its control key is deleted.

DELVD – Delete Variable Direct
A Variable record, identified by its relative position, is deleted.

WRITD – Write Direct
Data is written directly to the location (internal reference point) specified in one of the parameters. This function is designed for use by user written recovery programs that may need to rewrite information directly from the log.

WRITM – Write Master
A record specified by its control key is read and the elements named in the data-list are updated with the data in the program's data-area. The record is then rewritten.

WRITV – Write Variable
A record specified by its relative position is updated with the data defined by the data-list and data-area parameters. The record need not have been previously read by the user.

Control functions:

SINON – Sign-on
This function identifies which DBMOD is to be used, the access mode (Read Only or Update) and the logging options.

OPENX – Open Multiple
The data sets named in a list are opened in the modes specified (Shared Update, Exclusive Update, Read Only, etc).

CLOSX – Close Multiple
The data sets named in the list are closed.

SINOF – Sign Off
This indicates that the programmer has finished accessing the TOTAL database.

COMIT
This generates a checkpoint. A program may be rolled back to a COMIT checkpoint.

MARKL
This command enables the programmer to write a user record to the log file.

QUIET

In a multi-tasking environment this command quiesces the database. All updated buffers are rewritten and a 'QUIET' record is written to the log.

QMARK

This is equivalent to a QUIET followed by a MARKL.

RSTAT

This command allows the statistical information collected by TOTAL to be accessed.

5 Internals

The objectives of this chapter are to:

— explain the need for an understanding of DBMS internals by certain staff;

and for each of the five DBMSs to:

— describe how the DBMS interfaces with the operating system and the modes in which it may run;

— explain how the data structures are actually implemented on physical storage;

— summarise the different techniques provided for accessing the data;

— describe the buffering mechanism.

INTRODUCTION

The majority of the users of a DBMS do not need to concern themselves with the internal workings of the software. They are only concerned with the interfaces to the system so they can safely view it as a 'black box'. However there are some types of users who will benefit from some knowledge of how the system works:

— Database Designers
Staff who are responsible for designing the database, or a part of it, need to consider the performance of the application programs which will access it. An appreciation of how the data structures are implemented will enable them to make sensible design decisions

and arm themselves with some of the technical information required to estimate access times.

— Programmers
The productivity of experienced programmers may be increased if they understand how the software works. A more detailed understanding of how the data is actually accessed may help them to design more efficient programs, for example to avoid repeated access to the same record, and help to reduce errors. In order to thoroughly test programs it may be necessary to inspect the structure of the test database by examining a printed dump of the physical blocks of data on the database file. Such an inspection requires a knowledge of how the data is physically organised.

— System Software Programmers
The technical support staff need to know how the DBMS interfaces with the operating system in order to install and maintain the software. They need to understand how the data structures are implemented in case they are called upon to investigate any DBMS problems. Also, in order to tune the DBMS and the operating environment as a whole, an appreciation of the buffering mechanism of the DBMS is required.

— DBMS Selection Team
Personnel responsible for the appraisal of available DBMSs and the selection of one also need to consider the technical issues. They need to know how the software can be run on their computer and whether any modifications to the operating system are required. The interfaces with other software such as teleprocessing monitors, data dictionaries, report writers and query facilities should be considered. Even if such software is not currently in use or being considered, it is very likely that it will be used during the lifetime of the DBMS. If a large active database is to be supported, or is anticipated in the future, the DBMS will need to support multithreading or be re-entrant in order to provide adequate performance. In addition consideration needs to be given to the way in which the space on the database is used, freed and re-used. Poor space management can result in time consuming reorganisations resulting in high maintenance costs, and on a volatile database it can quickly have a dramatic effect on the performance.

DBMS INTERFACE TO THE OPERATING SYSTEM

This section describes the ways in which the five DBMSs may be interfaced with their host operating systems. There are two basic methods and all five DBMSs support both approaches. In the simplest method each batch program has its own copy of the DBMS software. Clearly the DBMS or operating system facilities must ensure that different copies of the DBMS do not try to share part of the database if updating is performed (this is discussed in the section on Multiple User Access in Chapter 3).

The second method allows one copy of the DBMS software to be shared by a number of batch and/or teleprocessing transaction programs. It is usually possible to specify the maximum number of programs which may be concurrently serviced by the DBMS. This is sometimes referred to as the number of threads and the term multithreading is used to describe the software's ability to concurrently service a number of threads or requests for service. The way in which the DBMS supports Multiple User Access is described in Chapter 3.

The following descriptions discuss the various modes in which the software can be executed. They explain how the software is loaded and whether the code is re-entrant or re-usable. Finally they indicate whether the source code and its associated documentation is available to the users.

ADABAS

ADABAS can be run in either the 'Single User Environment' or the 'Multi-User Environment'. In the Single User Environment (Figure 17) the database software is loaded into the application program's storage at run time. ADABAS guards against the possibility of multiple copies of itself simultaneously updating the database.

The 'Multi-User Environment' allows one copy of ADABAS to be shared by a number of batch and on-line users (Figure 18). While database services may be required it runs as a never-ending job which may be considered as a logical extension to the operating system's data management services. This single copy of the software can detect and control attempts to concurrently update the same record or file. Communication between the ADABAS nucleus running in one partition (or region, virtual machine, etc) and the applications running in other partitions is achieved by means of a special supervisor call.

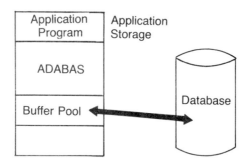

Figure 17   ADABAS Single User Environment

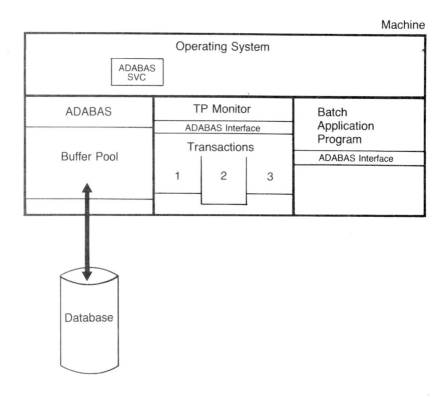

Figure 18   ADABAS Multi-User Environment

ADABAS, when used in the multi-user mode, multithreads both batch and on-line users. The maximum number of threads permitted is set at startup time. Update commands are not logically multithreaded against other updates (although the physical updates to the database are multi-threaded) as this would cause recovery difficulties. Retrieval commands are multithreaded against other retrieval commands and possibly an update command.

The software automatically gives teleprocessing users a higher priority than batch users in order to give them good response times. Similarly, requests from batch users which use simple search criteria are given priority.

Most of the database software is loaded dynamically at run time. Only one small interface module is actually link edited with the application program. The link edited program can be made completely independent of different releases of the software by using an interface called ADAHOOK.

There are only two modules which are operating system dependent. One of these modules handles input/output and operator specified functions, the other uses the ADABAS supervisor call for cross-partition (or region) communication. None of the other modules in the software uses any operating system services.

The source code of ADABAS and its related documentation is not available to users unless support for the software ceases.

DMS 1100

DMS 1100 is logically part of the operating system's data management software (Figure 19). It can be run in either a Single Threading or a Multi Threading Mode. In the latter mode DMS 1100 runs in common storage and is under the control of the system operator. Multiple copies of the system may be run concurrently as in a computer bureau environment but a given database may only be used by one copy. The Multi Threading version can support a number of batch and teleprocessing applications.

The DMS 1100 run time code, which is called the Data Management Routine (DMR), is fully re-entrant. Depending upon the configuration the DMR may optionally raise itself to a real time priority after it has been started. This allows on-line users to be given a good service. Each run-unit may assign itself a priority. The DMR rolls back the run-unit with the

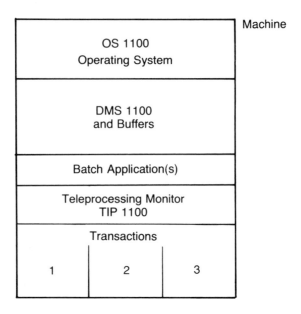

Figure 19   DMS 1100 Single/Multi Threading Mode

lowest priority when it is resolving a deadlock. There is no priority scheduling of run-units within the DMR. Since the DMR is re-entrant each run-unit executes the DMS 1100 code at its operating system priority.

Application programs do not have to contain any DMS 1100 coding which may be release dependent. A 'linker' routine may be collected (link edited) with each program using the database or it may be loaded dynamically at execution time. The linker routine handles the communications with the Data Management Routine. The DMR is loaded when it is first referenced and then normally remains resident until it is closed down.

The source code for DMS 1100 is provided. Program modules can be assembled/compiled during the installation and system generation procedures.

When the system is generated it is possible to omit modules which support facilities that are not required.

IDMS

IDMS can be run in either the 'Local Mode' or the 'Central Mode'. In the Local Mode the database software is loaded into the application program's storage at run time (Figure 20). The software protects the 'database' against multiple copies concurrently updating it by not allowing more than one application to open the same part of the database for update.

The 'Central' Version of IDMS allows a number of applications to share one copy of the software (Figure 21). This copy of IDMS runs as a never-ending job whilst database services are required. It can be considered as a logical extension to the operating system's data management services.

The Central Version allows a number of applications, which can include teleprocessing monitors, to concurrently update the database. The system locks records until an update sequence is complete and resolves deadlock situations. Communication between IDMS running in one partition (or region, virtual machine, etc) and the applications running in their own partitions is achieved by the use of a special supervisor call.

It is also possible to run the Central Version in two other modes when a teleprocessing monitor is in use. In both cases IDMS shares the same partition or region as the teleprocessing monitor. The database software can either run as a never-ending transaction under the control of the TP monitor or as an operating system task if multitasking is supported.

On ICL 2900 machines under the operating system VME (Virtual Machine Environment) IDMS can be run as either an 'Unshared Service' or as a 'Shared Service'. The 'Unshared Service' is equivalent to Local Mode (Figure 22). The operating system and the IDMS run time code is held in 'global storage' so that other virtual machines may use the same copy of the fully re-entrant code.

The 'Shared Service' is equivalent to the Central Version. It is started in its own virtual machine and services database requests from other virtual machines until it is closed down. A number of applications, including Application Virtual Machines running under a teleprocessing monitor, can concurrently update the database (Figure 23). The system locks parts of the database until an update sequence is complete and allows deadlock situations to be identified. The communication between

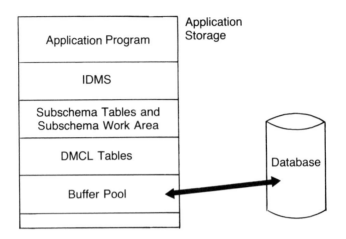

Figure 20   IDMS (Cullinane) Local Mode

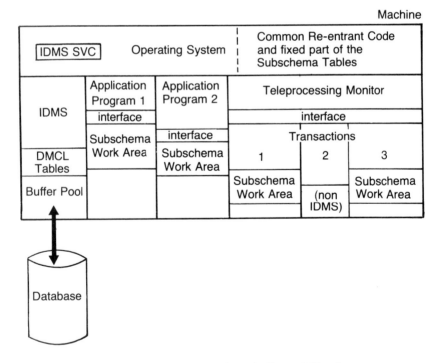

Figure 21   IDMS (Cullinane) Central Version

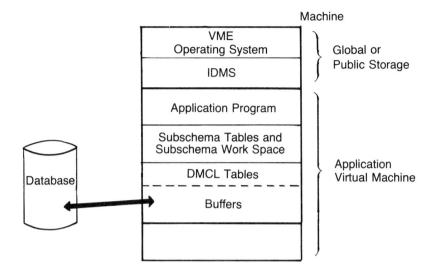

Figure 22   IDMS (ICL) Unshared Service

the virtual machines is achieved through the use of standard system facilities.

When IDMS is used in Central or Shared Service Mode it multithreads batch programs and on-line transaction programs. An active program is known as a run-unit. The maximum number of programs which may be concurrently active (threads) is set when the Central Version is generated. In ICL implementations the number of threads is specified in the Service Description Language.

The Central Version is capable of multithreading both multiple retrieval and multiple updates. The locking facilities are used to assure the logical integrity of the database in a concurrent updating environment. If required, a run-unit may request exclusive retrieval or update access to part of the database.

In the Cullinane Product it is possible to assign priorities to the programs, or run-units, running under the control of central version. The priorities may be changed dynamically at run time. There are also facilities for the console operator to cancel any selected run-unit should the need arise.

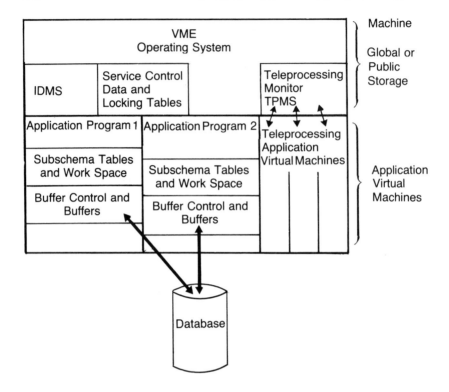

Figure 23   IDMS (ICL) Shared Service

In the ICL Product the architecture of the 2900 series of machines allows fully re-entrant IDMS code to be executed as if it were a user subroutine. Control does not have to be relinquished to a separately dispatched program as in the case of IBM equipment. Priorities are therefore determined by the operating system priority of the virtual machines using IDMS. When a number of users have to queue for a 'busy' resource the queue is processed in a first-come, first-served manner, multithreading the request where possible.

When the Cullinane version of IDMS is running in local mode the required modules are loaded into the application's storage when the database is opened. In the central mode the modules are loaded when the system is started. About 50% of the nucleus software is fully re-entrant and may be loaded into the operating system's shared program area, ie the OS Link Pack Area or DOS Shared Virtual Area. The basic database management software is not overlaid although one of the software's compilers is overlaid.

For unshared services of the ICL Product the subschema and DMCL tables are loaded at run time through the use of a service startup macro. The IDMS in-line code is normally loaded into public storage so that one copy of the re-entrant code can be used by all IDMS services. The required subschema table is loaded when the program opens the database. When a Shared Service is used the subschema is loaded into the application's local storage when the database is opened. The main portion of the DMCL table is loaded at startup time into global storage. A part of the DMCL table, including buffers, is created in each application's local storage.

The application program has a small interface module linked to it. At run time this interface dynamically loads the required modules. Some of these modules are fully re-entrant so they may be loaded into the operating system's common code area (the Link Pack area on OS systems or the Shared Virtual Area on DOS systems). The remaining code is serially reusable.

The Central Version of IDMS is a multitasking monitor in its own right. In fact it incorporates the nucleus of IDMS-DC, Cullinane's teleprocessing monitor. It includes many options for controlling, monitoring and tuning the system.

ICL's IDMS code for the 2900 version is fully re-entrant. In fact the architecture of the 2900 series of machines forces all code, including application programs, to be re-entrant.

All program code, including subroutines, can be cascade loaded (dynamically loaded at run time). If required the CALLed program code can be collected (link edited) with the application program although this is not recommended since it makes it more difficult to change to new releases of IDMS.

The source code for IDMS and the related program logic documentation is not available to users.

IMS-DL/1

DL/1 can be run in either local mode or central mode. When used in local

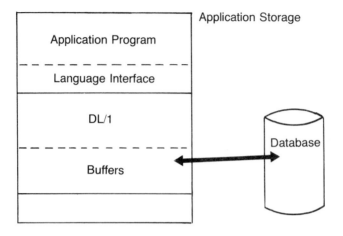

Figure 24 DL/1 Local Mode

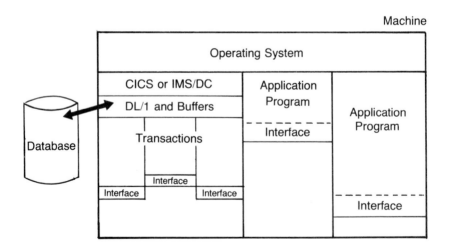

Figure 25 DL/1 Central Mode

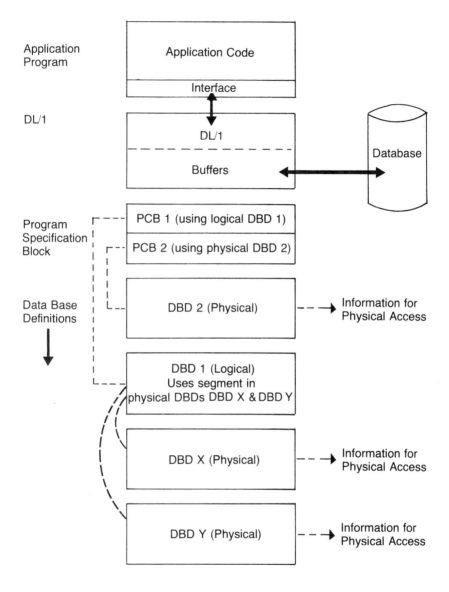

Figure 26   DL/1 Relationship between PSB, PCB, Logical DBD and Physical DBD

mode the database software and application program are loaded into a partition or region at run time (Figure 24). The database is protected against the possibility of multiple local copies of the database concurrently updating the database by job control language data set or VSAM file share options.

When DL/1 is used in central mode a number of on-line and batch users may concurrently access and update the database. In this mode DL/1 executes in the same partition as the teleprocessing system (Figure 25). Communication between a batch application program and the DL/1 software executing in another partition is achieved through the use of supervisor facilities.

Part of the code for DL/1 is re-entrant and may be loaded into the OS Link Pack Area or DOS Shared Virtual Area. The non re-entrant code is serially reusable. DL/1 allows multiple retrieval requests and multiple update requests to be multithreaded. Data integrity is protected by the locking mechanism. The processing priority of a task is determined by the task's priority within the operating or teleprocessing system. Internally DL/1 queues requests in a first-come first-served order.

A small interface program is link edited to each application to handle the communications with the DL/1 software. Other parts of the database software are loaded dynamically either at run time for the local mode, or at startup time for the central mode. Figure 26 illustrates how the PSB, PCBs, logical DBDs and physical DBDs are related.

Some of the DL/1 modules are re-entrant and may be loaded into the operating system's common code area. The non re-entrant code is serially reusable.

The source code and program logic documentation is freely available to licensees of DOS/VS DL/1 and IMS/VS.

TOTAL

When run under IBM operating systems, TOTAL can be run in these modes: Batch Mode, Multi-Task Batch Mode and Multi-Task TP Mode. In Batch Mode (equivalent to local, or single user mode) the database software is loaded into the application program's storage at run time (Figure 27). The Multi-Tasking Mode (equivalent to central version or a multi-user mode) supports a number of tasks in either different partitions or multi-tasking within one partition. When a teleprocessing monitor is

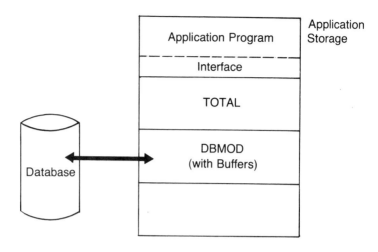

Figure 27 TOTAL Batch Mode

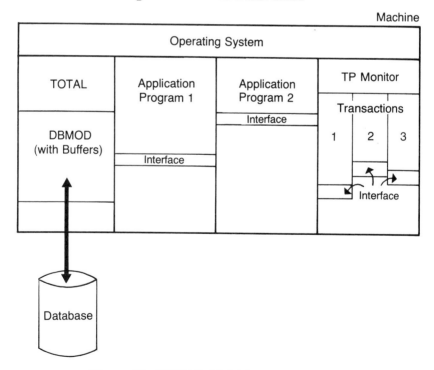

Figure 28   TOTAL Multi-Task Batch Mode

used TOTAL can run under its control in the Multi-Task TP Mode to take advantage of the close relationship between them.

When TOTAL is run in Central Mode (Multi-Task Batch Mode) one copy of the software is shared by either a number of batch or a number of on-line users, or possibly both, depending on the TP monitor used (Figure 28). The software runs as a never-ending job and may be considered as a logical extension of the operating system's data management services. It can detect and control attempts to concurrently update the same record.

When TOTAL is servicing teleprocessing users, the software runs in the storage controlled by the teleprocessing monitor (Figure 29). It runs as a separate task which will normally be started when the on-line system is started and continues running until the on-line system is closed down. TOTAL may run as a separate operating system task, ie using subtasking, so that it may be multiprogrammed with the teleprocessing system functions. Alternatively it may run as a never-ending teleprocessing transaction and rely on the multiprogramming capabilities of the teleprocessing monitor.

The TOTAL code is serially re-usable. When it is used in the multi-task mode requests are multithreaded. Multiple retrieval and multiple update

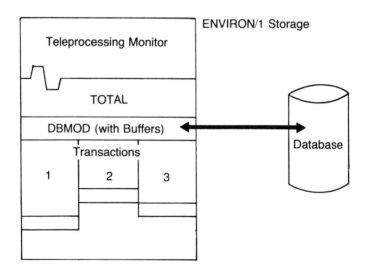

Figure 29   TOTAL Multi-Task TP Mode

requests can be multithreaded. The record locking facilities prevent a record being simultaneously updated by multiple users.

There are no facilities for assigning priorities to threads. When a number of commands, one per thread, are being processed together TOTAL will give priority to the command that arrived earliest which is not waiting for I/O.

A small TOTAL interface module is link edited with each application program using the database. This interface simply loads the TOTAL nucleus on the first call so that no release dependent code is link edited to the program. Other parts of the database software are loaded dynamically either at run time for the local mode, or at startup time for the central mode.

The source code for TOTAL and its related documentation is not made available to the users unless support ceases to be available from the vendor.

THE PHYSICAL IMPLEMENTATION OF DATA STRUCTURES

The aim of this section is to describe the physical organisations of the five DBMSs. It includes a discussion of the files needed to support a database together with a description of their organisation and details of their management of free space. The descriptions also illustrate, in detail, how pointer chains, indexes and inverted indexes are used to implement the various logical structures supported by the five systems.

ADABAS

ADABAS normally requires four operating system data sets (Figure 30). The ASSOCIATOR data set contains control information which describes the database. The DATA STORAGE data set holds the actual data. A DATA PROTECTION FILE is used to log database changes and enable recovery in the event of a failure. Fast recovery, called automatic rollback, uses a WORK FILE.

The Associator contains the control information for the database. It holds the File and Field Description Tables which contain detailed information about the record format of each file and the name, length and data format of every field within a record. The Association Network and Address Converter, which are used to address records stored in Data Storage, are also kept in the Associator.

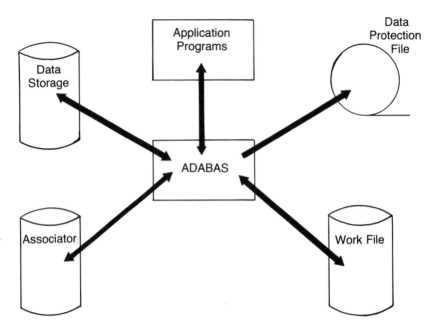

Figure 30   ADABAS

ADABAS uses inverted lists to permit data to be retrieved on various keys known as descriptor fields. For every descriptor field in the database ADABAS builds and maintains an inverted list which is stored in an area of the Associator called the ASSOCIATION NETWORK. The inverted list for a descriptor has an entry for every value that the field actually takes in the database. These descriptor values are ordered in ascending sequence.

Each descriptor value entry has a list of the identities of all the records in the field which contain the descriptor value (Figure 31).

This list consists of 'ISNs', Internal Sequence Numbers, which are logical pointers or database keys. When a record is added to the database it is assigned an ISN which it retains until the record is deleted. The physical block containing the record with a given ISN is identified by use of the 'ADDRESS CONVERTER'.

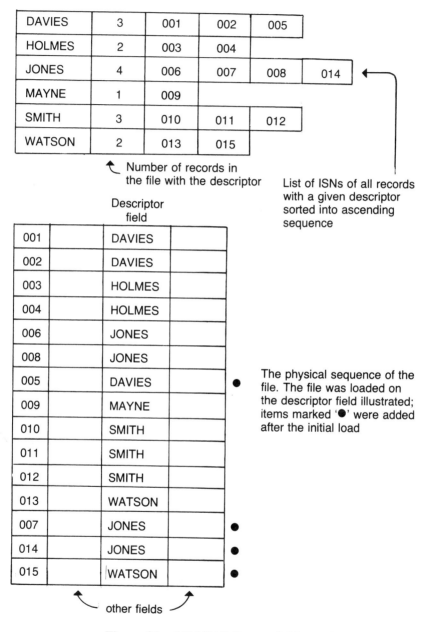

Figure 31   ADABAS Inverted List

The Address Converter consists of a table of logical block numbers. The ISN is used to index into this table. The table entry then identifies which block within the direct access file contains the required record. Once this block has been read into storage the ISNs of the records it contains are examined until the record is located (Figure 32).

If the physical position of a record changes for any reason the system only needs to amend the entry in the Address Converter. Any inverted lists referring to the record are insulated from the change by the address mapping. The size of the Address Converter is determined by the maximum number of records that can be stored in the file.

A physical block will normally contain a number of logical database records. Each record in the block is prefixed by its length and its ISN. ADABAS normally compresses data fields by not storing empty fields, leading zeros and trailing blanks, although this may be overridden. Fields which have been compressed are prefixed by their length. A field is identified by its relative sequence in the record, so null (empty) fields must be accounted for (Figure 32). Notice that records do not contain any pointer fields.

In order to permit efficient access to, and maintenance of, the inverted lists, ADABAS uses a hierarchical indexing mechanism. The index may have from three to five levels.

The ADABAS Data Storage data set is a formatted direct access file. Each ADABAS logical file defined is allocated a number of blocks from the Data Storage data set. The number of blocks allocated is determined by the Data Base Administrator, using information produced by a Load Utility, and it is based upon the number of records that are to be stored in the file. This information is stored in a control block for the file in the Associator.

A physical block normally holds a number of records in their compressed form. At database load time records are stored from the start of the file, each block being filled to a specified percentage of its capacity. The amount of free space left in each block is recorded in the Associator. The data within a block is never fragmented. If a record is deleted any following records in the affected block are moved up so that all the free space is contiguous at the end of the block.

When a record is to be added to the file ADABAS searches a Free Space Table, which is part of the Associator, to find a block which will

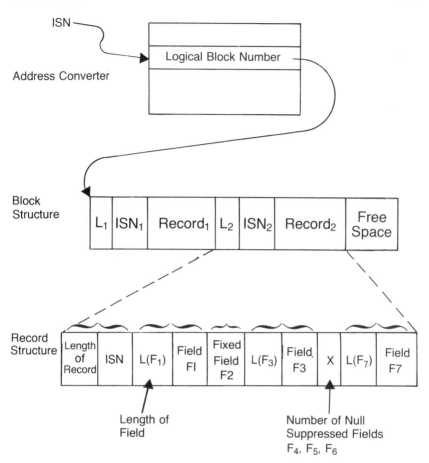

Figure 32   ADABAS Address Converter and Record Structure

accommodate the new record. If no space can be found ADABAS attempts to allocate 25% more space for the file from free space in Data Storage. Such secondary allocations can occur up to four times for each file.

If a record is updated and as a result its length increases it may not be possible to return it to the same physical block. In this case the record is removed from the original block and stored in a block where space is available. Only the record's logical block number will change in the

File A to File B Coupling Table

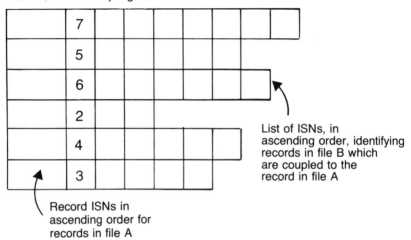

Record ISNs in
ascending order for
records in file A

List of ISNs, in
ascending order, identifying
records in file B which
are coupled to the
record in file A

File B to File A Coupling Table

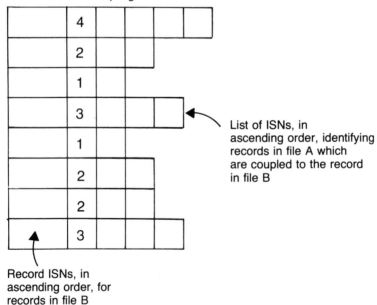

Record ISNs, in
ascending order, for
records in file B

List of ISNs, in
ascending order, identifying
records in file A which
are coupled to the record
in file B

Figure 33a   ADABAS Coupling Tables

Coupling Tables:

Parts to Supplier coupling

8145	1	9246		
8185	1	9522		
8212	2	9321	9522	
8346	3	9246	9321	9522
8765	2	9321	9522	

Supplier to Parts coupling

9246	2	8145	8346		
9321	3	8212	8346	8765	
9522	4	8185	8212	8346	8765

Parts File:

ISN   part #   part data

8145	2621	
8212	2987	
8346	4313	
8185	5444	
8765	6311	

Supplier File:

ISN   supplier #   supplier data   part #

9246	098		4313
			2621
9321	165		6311
			4313
			2987
9522	432		4313
			2987
			6311
			5444

Multiple
Field
identifies
parts which
can be
supplied

Note: There will probably be inverted lists for
    part # in the Parts file and
    supplier # in the Supplier file

Figure 33b   Coupling Example

address converter. The Association Network will be unaffected by the change of location since its ISN does not change.

File coupling relationships are implemented by using two tables. In a coupling relation two files are linked through a common descriptor field, that is a field which occurs in both files. The coupling tables are inverted lists but instead of using descriptor values as keys they use record ISNs (Figure 33a). For a given record in one file these tables allow all records in the other file with the same common descriptor to be identified.

Suppose for example that File A is a Parts File and File B is the Supplier File and that they are coupled on the common field Part Number (Figure 33b). Then for a given part the coupling table for File A/B identifies all the suppliers of the part in the Supplier File (B). Conversely, from the coupling table for File B/A, we can determine which parts come from a given Supplier.

ADABAS also supports a sparse indexing facility. This allows index entries to be maintained for only specified values of a field. 'Super-descriptors' are used to implement this facility.

A superdescriptor is a descriptor which is constructed for more than one field. Index entries are not maintained for superdescriptors which contain a NULL element so one of the fields comprising the superdescriptor can be used to select the values to be indexed.

DMS 1100

A DMS 1100 database consists of one or more operating system files which can be accessed directly. These files are formatted with physical blocks which are called PAGES. A PAGE is the basic unit of transfer between main memory and secondary storage. The collection of PAGES in an operating system file is termed an AREA. There is a one to one relationship between an AREA and an operating system file (see Figure 34).

There are three different types of AREA. A DATA AREA holds data records. An INDEX AREA holds the index for a record type whose mode is Indexed Sequential or an indexed pointer array set. A POINTER AREA is used to hold pointer arrays for a set. The page size and number of pages per Area are specified for each Area in the schema.

A database RECORD is stored on a PAGE. Each record on a PAGE is

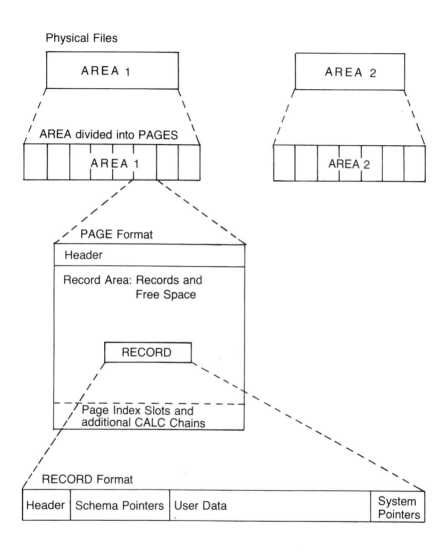

Figure 34   DMS 1100 Physical Organisation of the Data

assigned a 'record-number', which is unique within the page, when the record is first stored. The combination of an Area identifier, page number within the given Area (relative block number) and the record-number produces a unique identifier for each record which is called a DATA-BASE KEY. When a record is added to the database it is assigned a database key which uniquely identifies it until it is deleted or reorganised.

Records of different types may be stored in the same AREA and may exist on the same PAGE. A given record type may be stored in a number of different AREAs if this has been specified in the schema. Each page has a header which contains information about overflow pages and page usage. A page index and optional calc chain fields are stored at the bottom of the page.

Each record has a header which indicates its record type, its length and whether it has been deleted. This is followed by pointer fields which are used to implement the various data structures. These pointer fields are followed by the user data. There may also be some system pointers at the end of the record.

Logical relationships between records are implemented by linking records together by database pointers, either as chains of records or through the use of an index. A database pointer is the concatenation of the area-number, page-number and slot-number. Whereas a record's database key does not change (except possibly as a result of a reorganis-ation) its database pointer can change. Suppose that the length of a record is modified and it cannot be rewritten to the same page. The record is stored on an overflow page and a database pointer to it is put into the page index entry addressed by its database key.

The Figures 35 to 37 illustrate how a set relationship may be implemented as a chain, a pointer array or an indexed pointer array. Once the required owner record has been located, possibly by the use of a calc key, its associated members can be accessed by following the pointer chain.

An Indexed Sequential access mode is also supported. Indexed Sequential records must be sorted into their logical sequence before they are loaded. During the load they are stored physically sequential through the area. An index is built in an index area, which has an entry for each page used, indicating the last key on the page.

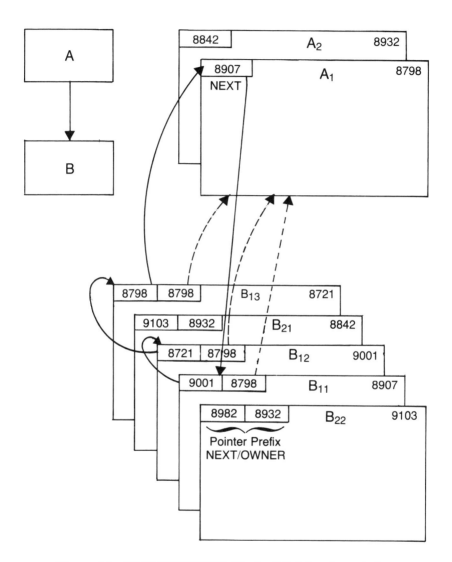

Figure 35   DMS 1100/IDMS Chained Set Implementation

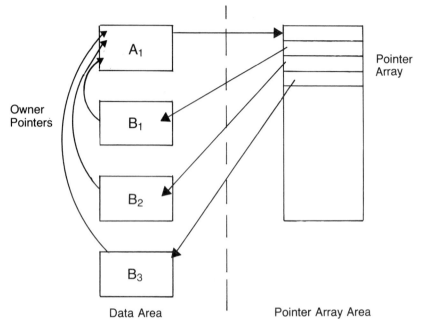

Figure 36   DMS 1100 Pointer Array Set Implementation

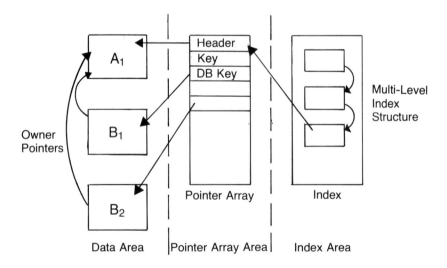

Figure 37   DMS 1100 Index Pointer Array Set Implementation

When a record type is defined in the schema it is given one of four location modes, namely 'CALC', 'VIA', 'DIRECT' or 'INDEX SEQUENTIAL'. These location modes determine how the record is stored in the database.

A 'CALC' record has a key field. This key is processed by a hashing algorithm in order to generate a page address within the allowed range for the record, where the system will try to store the record. CALC records will therefore be distributed randomly throughout the areas to which they are allocated.

Members of a set can be stored 'VIA' their owner record type. The system attempts to cluster member records around a logical insertion point. This may be around their owner or a point in a different area.

Records with the 'DIRECT' mode are assigned a database key by the application program. If the system cannot store the record in the requested position, because the target page is full or the database key is already assigned to another record, DMS 1100 returns an error response code to the program.

INDEX SEQUENTIAL records are initially loaded so that they are physically sequential. An index is constructed, in an index area, which has an entry for each page used containing the key of the last record on that page (Figure 38). Once the index has been created it is not updated. New

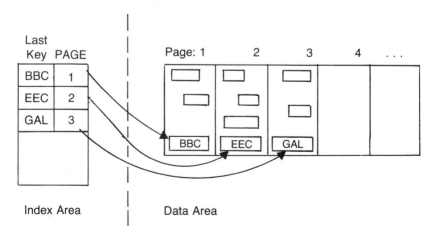

Figure 38   DMS 1100 Index Sequential Access

data records are stored on the page indicated by the index. Existing records on the page are moved down if necessary in order to maintain the correct physical sequence of the record. If the target page is full an error condition is signalled unless linkages have been allocated for overflow management.

Additional access keys are implemented as singular indexed pointer array sets.

If DMS 1100 cannot place a record on its target page the system will use its space management routines to find a free space within the database. When a record is deleted from the database, it is not physically removed; it is flagged as being deleted. Consequently, the free space on a page may become fragmented. Should the system discover that it cannot store a record on a page it will compact the page by relocating records up the page, thereby physically deleting the logically deleted records, so all the free space will be contiguous at the bottom of the page. Free entries in the page index, resulting from deletions, are reused when records are added to the page.

When a record which is to be deleted has two or more owners it has to be unlinked from all the sets in which it participates. If any of these sets do not have both next and prior pointers, the record is unlinked by reading round the set in order to relink the chain past the deleted record.

If the system cannot place a record on its target page because the page is full, the space management routines make use of overflow pages. An area may optionally be defined to have either a number of global overflow pages at the end of the area or a number of interspersed overflow pages spaced throughout the area, or possibly both. If a page overflows, the system locates the next interspersed overflow pages and attempts to store the record. If no interspersed overflow pages exist, or if they are full, the system will attempt to store the record on the global overflow pages if any exist. The system will repeat this search for each area in which the record may be stored. If no space can be found an error response code is returned to the user.

An area may be defined as EXPANDABLE up to a specified maximum number of pages. This allows additional pages to be allocated to the area at some future date without having to unload and reload the data. It is also possible to define the area as DYNAMICALLY EXPANDABLE up to a specified maximum number of pages. In this case overflow pages

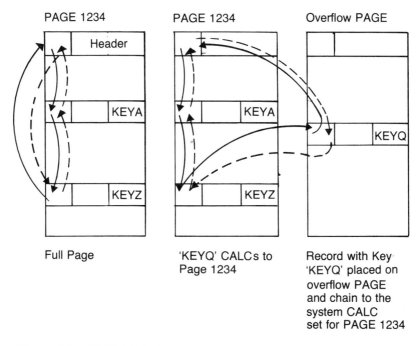

Figure 39   DMS 1100 Overflow Management for CALC Records

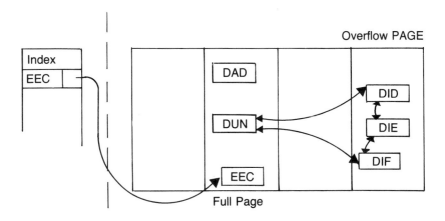

Figure 40   DMS 1100 Overflow Management for Index Sequential Records

are allocated dynamically when a target page becomes full. The overflow page is reserved for that target page so subsequent overflow can be handled efficiently.

Records with a storage mode of 'CALC' which are stored on overflow pages must be linked to their target page in order to be retrievable. DMS 1100 uses an internal system CALC set to achieve this. Every page is considered to be the owner of one, or more, system CALC sets. All CALC records are linked to their target page by a system CALC set as shown in Figure 39. To retrieve a record, the system searches the CALC set for a record of the correct type having the required key. A system CALC set can optionally have prior pointers.

If an area is defined with a number of system CALC sets the hashing algorithm generates a target page and a target system CALC chain identifier. This facility is used to avoid long CALC chains which could degrade performance.

Records with a mode of INDEX SEQUENTIAL may be stored on overflow pages if NEXT and PRIOR linkages have been allocated. The new record is stored on an overflow page and linked to the record on the target page which logically follows it as illustrated in Figure 40.

Variable length records are never fragmented. If a record increases its length as a result of an update it is relocated into overflow if the original page can no longer accommodate it.

IDMS

An IDMS database consists of one or more operating system direct access FILES. These files are formatted with physical blocks which are called PAGEs. Each page in the database has a unique 'page-number' which is used by the direct access method to locate it. A PAGE is the basic unit of data transfer between main memory and secondary storage (see Figure 41).

The PAGEs in the database are grouped together into one or more database AREAs. An AREA can be considered as a logical file containing PAGEs of the same size and having a contiguous and sequential range of page-numbers. The PAGEs comprising an AREA are mapped, by the Schema definition, into one or more FILES; a FILE may contain one or more AREAs.

Physical Files

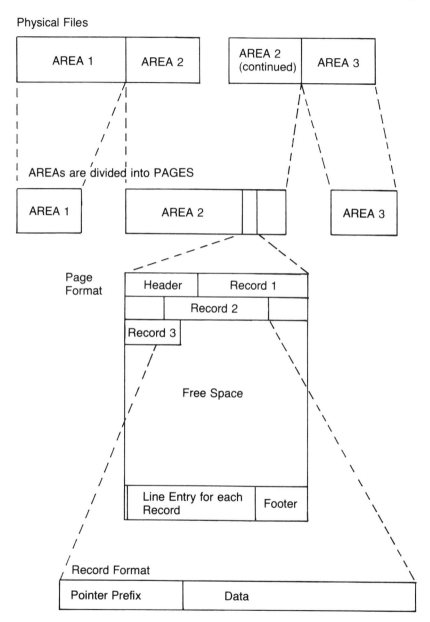

Figure 41   IDMS Physical Data Organisation

A database RECORD is stored on a PAGE. Each record on a PAGE is assigned a 'line-number', which is unique within the page, when the record is first stored. The combination of the page-number and the line-number produces a unique identifier for every record in the database called a database key. When a record is added to the database it is assigned a database key which uniquely identifies it until it is deleted or re-organised. Records of different types may be stored within an AREA and exist on the same PAGE.

Every page has a Page Header, a Page Footer and a Line Index. The Header and Footer contain the Page number, details about available free space and other control information. The Line Index contains an entry for every record on the page; it identifies the record type, length of the prefix, length of the data portion and where the record is located on the page. The record prefix contains the chain fields used to implement logical relationships.

The logical relationships between records can be implemented as chains of records linked together by pointers as shown in Figure 35. Database keys are used as the pointers although these are transparent to the programmer. Once the required owner record has been located, its associated member records can be accessed by following the chain of pointers. The owner record would typically be located by using the 'CALC' storage/retrieval mode.

Indexes may be set up for any record type. This facility causes a record to be stored following and as close as possible to the previously stored record of the same type. An index is set up of the record type symbolic keys and the associated database keys of the record. These indexes are searched, using a binary chop technique, to locate a record. They can also be used to access the data sequentially. If an index block becomes full another level of index is constructed by the system (Figure 42). Utilities are provided for maintaining these indexes.

An IDMS record may be given one of three location modes when it is defined in the schema, namely 'CALC', 'VIA' or 'DIRECT'. These location modes determine how the record is stored in the database.

In the 'CALC' mode, a field within the record type is defined as a key. IDMS uses a hashing algorithm on this key to generate a page address where it will try to locate the record. CALC records will therefore be randomly distributed throughout the AREA containing them.

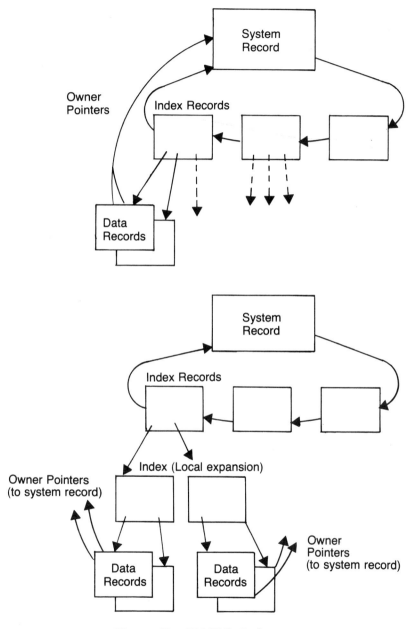

Figure 42   IDMS Indexing

Member record types can be stored 'VIA' their owner record type. The system attempts to cluster the member records on the same page(s), often around their owner. This will reduce the number of physical input/output operations needed to read the records in the set.

The 'DIRECT' mode allows the user to suggest on which page the record should be stored. The system will store the record on, or close to, the suggested page and return the database key to the user. This mode is not widely used.

Space on an IDMS page is never fragmented. When a record is stored it is placed so that it follows any existing data at the top of the page. A line index entry for the record is built at the bottom of the page. Records are relocated up the page so that all the free space is contiguous when a record cannot be stored on the page because the space is fragmented.

If the record being deleted has two or more owners it is not possible to physically delete the complete record without unlinking it from all the sets in which it participates. If these sets do not have both next and prior pointers it would be necessary to read round them in order to relink the chain past the deleted record. In order to avoid such a potentially time consuming operation IDMS flags the record as logically deleted. A logically deleted record, which consists of just the record prefix, will be physically deleted when it is unlinked from the last set in which it participates. Alternatively, a utility can be used to remove logically deleted records.

If the system cannot place a fixed length record on its target page the space management algorithm finds a page in the Area which will accommodate it. IDMS reserves 'Space Management Pages' at intervals throughout each Area (Figure 43). Space management pages hold information about the available space in the pages that follow it. In order to reduce the number of accesses to the space management page the available space information is only updated while a page is more than 70% full; it is reset to 'empty' if a deletion causes it to fall below this figure.

When the system discovers that a new record will not fit on its target page the preceding space management page is scanned to find a page, following the target page, which should have enough free space to hold the record. If no space is found the following space management pages are accessed, looping round at the end of the Area if necessary, until a suitable page is found. Should the starting point be reached the pro-

Figure 43   IDMS Space Management Pages

grammer will be passed a return code which indicates that there is no room to store the record anywhere in the Area.

If a variable length record cannot be stored in its entirety on the target page the system can split it into a root and a number of fragments, as shown in Figure 44. Minimum permitted sizes of both the root and the fragments can be specified in the Schema. When a variable length record is stored the system tries to place the whole record on the target page. If it will not fit, it attempts to store a root fragment on the target page and the remainder of the record on subsequent pages. If the root fragment will not fit onto the target page a suitable page is found by space management. When a variable length record is accessed and the Area has been opened for update the system will automatically try to eliminate or reduce the fragmentation.

Records with a storage mode of CALC which cannot be stored on their target page need to be related to their target page in order to allow them to be retrieved by their key. IDMS uses an internal 'System CALC Set' to deal with this problem (Figure 45). Every page is considered to have a 'System CALC Set' owner record which has any record that 'CALCs' to its page as a member. When a record of a given record type and with a given key is to be retrieved the system searches its CALC Set by examining the keys of those records of the appropriate type. The owner of the system CALC Set is part of the page header. This Set has next and prior pointers and is sorted into ascending sequence on the record keys.

Some implementations allow any record type, irrespective of location mode, to have any number of additional access keys defined through indexes (Figure 46). These keys allow random access and sequential processing by key. The index sequence may be specified as either ascending or descending. Duplicate records may be either not allowed or ordered first, last or by their database key. Access to a record type may be optimised for sequential key processing by using the location mode

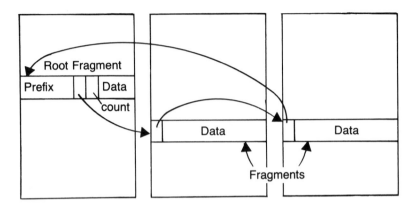

Figure 44   IDMS Fragmentation of Variable Length Records

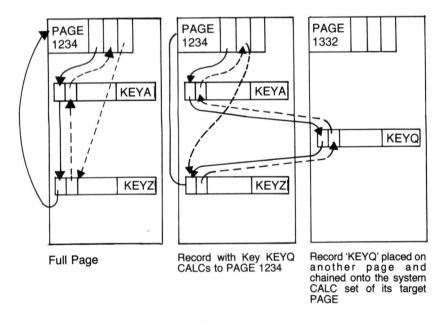

Figure 45   IDMS Overflow Management of CALC Records

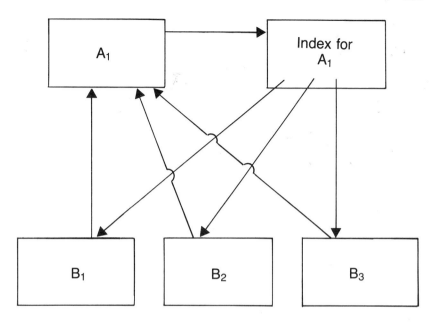

Figure 46   IDMS Indexing

SEQUENTIAL. This ensures that records are placed in their physical sequence in the database AREA at load time.

They also allow a set to be implemented using an index rather than by chaining member records together. The index is linked to the owner record and each member has an owner pointer. The index records are treated like user-defined record types by the system, and their placement can be specified in the schema. If the addition of records causes an index block to become full a local expansion of the index hierarchy occurs. An additional index level is created for the records in the index block that has been filled.

IMS-DL/1

A DL/1 database consists of one or more operating system data sets. In general each data set has a one-to-one correspondence with a physical database described by a Data Base Description (DBD).

A number of access methods are supported. The access method to be used to access a physical database (file) is specified in its DBD. The major DL/1 access methods are:

— Simple Hierarchical Sequential Access Method (SHSAM);

— Hierarchical Sequential Access Method (HSAM);

— Simple Hierarchical Indexed Sequential Access Method (SHISAM);

— Hierarchical Indexed Sequential Access Method (HISAM);

— Hierarchical Direct Access Method (HDAM);

— Hierarchical Indexed Direct Access Method (HIDAM).

These access methods are described below. The DL/1 access methods can be implemented using either the Virtual Storage Access Method (VSAM) Key and Entry Sequence Data Sets (KSDS and ESDS), or the Indexed Sequential Access Method (ISAM) and the Overflow Sequential Access Method (OSAM). The descriptions that follow only make reference to VSAM KSDS and ESDS access methods in order to avoid unnecessary complications and to reflect IBM's emphasis on VSAM.

SHSAM

A SHSAM physical database (file) holds a physical database record type that consists of just one segment type, ie the root (see Figure 47). Segments are loaded and read serially (physically sequentially). They cannot be updated. The operating system sequential access methods are used as the basis for SHSAM. A SHSAM physical database may be stored on disk or tape.

HSAM

A HSAM physical database (file) holds a hierarchical physical database record type (see Figure 48). The records are loaded and read serially (physically sequentially). Once the records have been loaded they cannot be updated. Each segment carries a prefix which identifies its type.

The operating system sequential access methods are also used as a basis for HSAM. A HSAM physical database may be stored on a disk or tape. Segments are loaded serially into the file's physical blocks. When a block

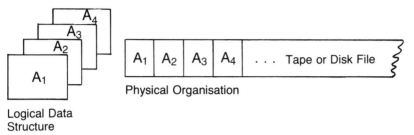

Logical Data
Structure

Physical Organisation

Figure 47   DL/1 SHSAM

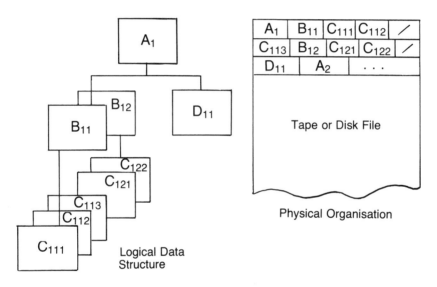

Figure 48   DL/1 HSAM

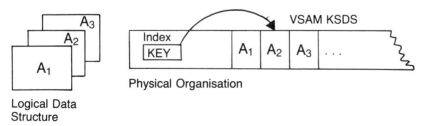

Logical Data
Structure

Physical Organisation

Figure 49   DL/1 SHISAM

does not contain enough free space to accommodate a segment the free space is filled with binary zeros and a new block is started.

SHISAM

A SHISAM physical database (file) holds a physical database record type consisting of just one segment type, ie the root, which contains a key field (see Figure 49). Segments can be read sequentially in ascending key order or accessed directly by their key. Segments may be added, deleted or modified. SHISAM is implemented as a VSAM KSDS. It is provided as a migration aid from VSAM to DL/1. VSAM space management allows space released by a deletion to be reused.

HISAM

A HISAM physical database (file) holds a hierarchical physical database record type (see Figure 50). Records may be accessed sequentially in ascending key order or directly by the key field in the root segment. Segments may be added, deleted or modified. Each segment carries a prefix which identifies its type.

A HISAM physical database (file) is implemented as a VSAM KSDS and a VSAM ESDS. The KSDS contains one entry for each root record occurrence. As many of the record's segments as possible are stored in the KSDS record. If more space is required one or more ESDS records are used to accommodate the overflow. The KSDS record and the related ESDS records are linked together by pointers.

Space management is handled partly in VSAM and partly by DL/1. The KSDS is managed by VSAM. DL/1 maintains the pointer in the KSDS record and the allocation of the ESDS records. When a segment is added or deleted DL/1 will move the existing segments of a structure occurrence so that their physical order reflects the logical order. ESDS records will be allocated/released to accommodate a database record whose number of segments increases/decreases as required. Space released by deletions can always be reused.

HDAM

A HDAM physical database (file) holds a hierarchical physical database record type (see Figure 51). Record occurrences can be accessed serially (physically sequentially) or directly by randomising the key defined for

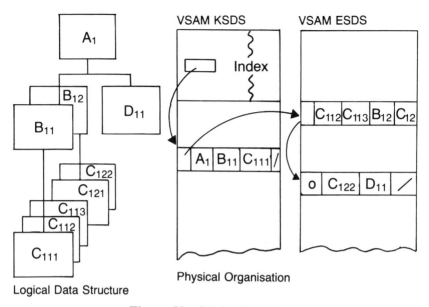

Figure 50   DL/1 HISAM

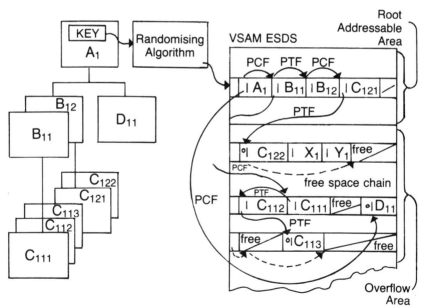

Figure 51   DL/1 HDAM – Physical Child and Twin Pointers

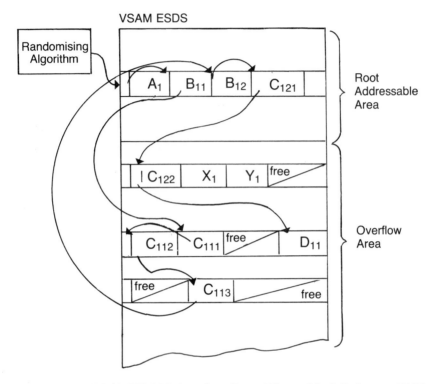

Figure 51   DL/1 HDAM (continued) – Hierarchical Pointers (IMS only)

the root segment. Unlike SHSAM, HSAM, SHISAM and HISAM where the physical layout of a segment reflects its logical layout, HDAM uses pointers to relate segments together in the correct manner. Each segment carries a prefix which identifies its type and contains the pointers. Segments may be added, deleted or modified. Space released by a deletion may be reused.

There are two ways of implementing the pointers. The physical child and the physical twin pointers allow segment occurrences of a given type to be accessed serially. Hierarchical pointers (IMS/VS only) relate the segments in their hierarchical sequence. Only one of these can be used to relate a parent and child but both may appear in a hierarchy, ie the pointers relating segments A and B can be physical child/twin while those relating segments B and C may be hierarchical.

A HDAM physical database (file) is implemented as one VSAM ESDS which is logically split into a Root Addressable Area and an Overflow area. The root addressable area contains root segments and a specified number of dependent segments. When a structure occurrence needs more space than the limit specified for the root addressable area the remaining segments are stored in the overflow area. Individual segments are always linked together by pointers so the ESDS records containing a structure occurrence do not need to be linked together explicitly.

Space within the VSAM ESDS is managed by DL/1. A bit map associated with the ESDS is used to indicate which ESDS records have sufficient free space to accommodate the largest segment in the structure. Within each ESDS record free space is chained together.

When a segment is added it is stored as close to its related segments as possible. If the segment cannot be placed within a specified distance of its related segments it is stored at the end of the file. When a segment is deleted the released space is added to the free space chain; the remaining segments are not relocated automatically by the system. When the HDAM physical database is loaded free space may be allocated to accommodate future updates.

HIDAM

A HIDAM physical database (file) holds a hierarchical physical database record type (see Figure 52). Record occurrences may be accessed sequentially in ascending key sequence or directly using the key of the root segment. HIDAM, like HDAM, uses physical child/twin or hierarchical (IMS only) pointers to relate segments together so the physical order of segments does not reflect the logical view of a record. Each segment has a prefix which identifies its type and contains the pointers. Segments may be added, deleted or modified.

HIDAM uses a VSAM KSDS and a VSAM ESDS. The data in the KSDS consists of a pointer to the root segment in the ESDS. Related segments within the ESDS are linked together by pointers. VSAM manages the free space within the KSDS. Free space within the ESDS is managed by DL/1 using the bit map and free space chain techniques used for HDAM.

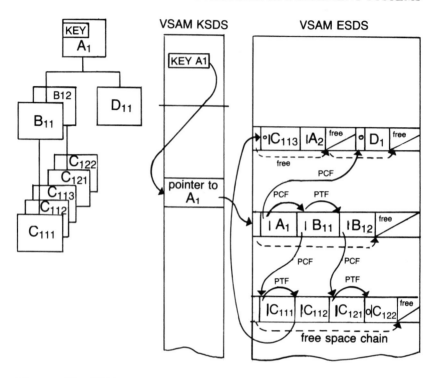

**Figure 52   HIDAM – Physical Child/Twin Pointers Illustrated
(Hierarchical pointers may be used under IMS)**

THE IMPLEMENTATION OF SEGMENT RELATIONSHIPS

The DL/1 sequential access methods (SHSAM, HSAM, SHISAM and
HISAM) require the segments of a physical database record to be physically ordered to reflect the logical structure. The direct access methods
(HDAM and HIDAM) use pointers to allow related segments to be
accessed in their logical sequence as shown in Figure 53. Four types of
pointers may be used:

— physical child (first) pointer (PCF);

— physical child last pointer (PCL);

— physical twin (forward) pointer (PTF);

— physical twin backward pointer (PTB).

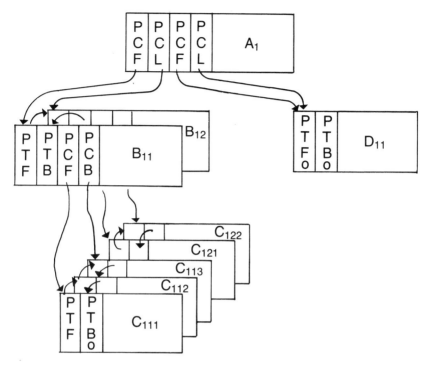

Figure 53   DL/Physical Pointers

UNIDIRECTIONAL RELATIONSHIPS

When a logical database record type contains segment types from differ-ent physical databases, pointers or symbolic keys are used to link related segments together. Suppose that initially there are two physical data-bases, and a logical database record type containing segments from each physical database is required as shown in Figure 54. This could be implemented as illustrated in Figure 55.

The segment type X′ is called a Logical Child. It has two parents; the physical parent segment type A and the logical parent segment type X. The logical child segment contains a pointer to the Target Segment as illustrated in Figure 56. When the logical child is accessed it contains the "logical parent concatenated key". If the segment contains data this is returned with the key. Such data is known as intersection data.

Existing Physical Databases:

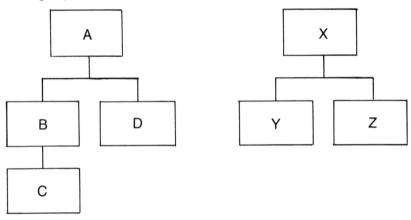

Required logical hierarchy contains segments from both physical databases:

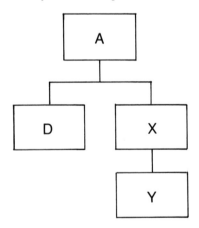

Figure 54   DL/1 Logical Databases

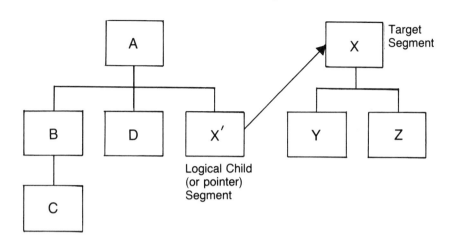

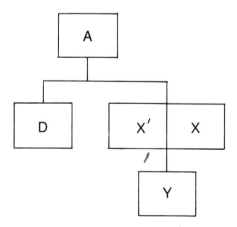

Figure 55   DL/1 Logical Child Segment

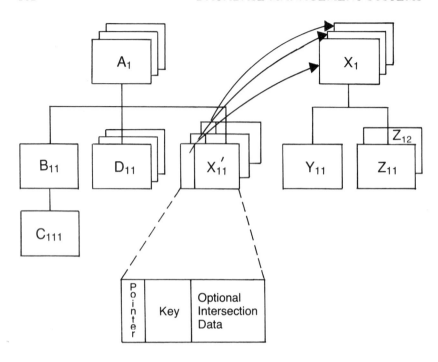

Figure 56   DL/1 Intersection Data

BIDIRECTIONAL RELATIONSHIPS (IMS/VS only)

In a unidirectional relationship there is a one way relationship between the logical child (pointer segment) and the logical parent (target segment). A bidirectional relationship is created if the logical parent is made to point back to its logical children.

Bidirectional relationships are implemented by use of the following pointers:

— Physical Parent pointers	(PP)	Mandatory
— Logical Parent pointers	(LP)	Mandatory
— Logical Child First pointers	(LCF)	Mandatory
— Logical Child Last pointers	(LCL)	Optional
— Logical Twin (Forward) pointers	(LTF)	Mandatory
— Logical Twin Backward pointers	(LTB)	Optional

Under IMS the Logical Parent pointer may, optionally, be symbolic. The logical parent's concatenated key may be stored in the logical child segment and used to address the logical parent.

Figure 57 is a revised version of Figure 56 to illustrate these bidirectional relationship pointers. The use of bidirectional relationships enables the logical database record type shown in Figure 58 to be accessed. This record type could have been specified by defining a unidirectional relationship as shown in Figure 59. In fact a bidirectional relationship is generated by defining both X' and A' as Logical Children. However, the bidirectional relationship can be maintained without the physical existence of A' so it is called a Virtual Logical Child. The segment type X' is sometimes called a Real Logical Child.

If both X' and A' were defined as Real Logical Children the relationship would be Bidirectional-Physical Paired. It is the user's responsibility to ensure that the inter-section data in X' and A' corresponds during loading but DL/1 manages it thereafter. When X' is a Real Logical Child and A' is a Virtual Logical Child, or vice-versa, the relationship is Bidirectional-Virtually Paired. Performance considerations determine which type of relationship should be used. Retrieval and update activity along the logical and physical paths must be considered.

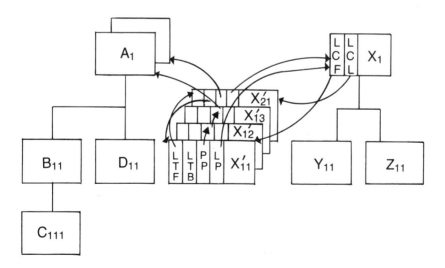

Figure 57   DL/1 Bidirectional Pointers

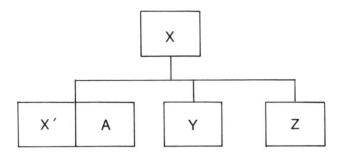

Figure 58   DL/1 Alternative Logical Database

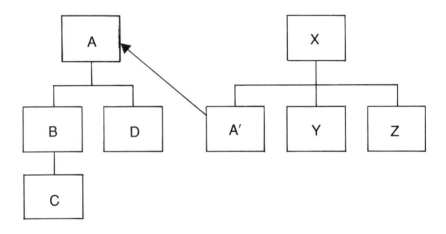

Figure 59   DL/1 Alternative Logical Child A′

SECONDARY INDEXING

Secondary indexing allows database records to be processed directly or sequentially by a key other than the root key. The segment that the index points to is called the Index Target Segment. However the actual key can be contained in the Target Segment or one of its dependents; the segment containing the key is called the Index Source Segment.

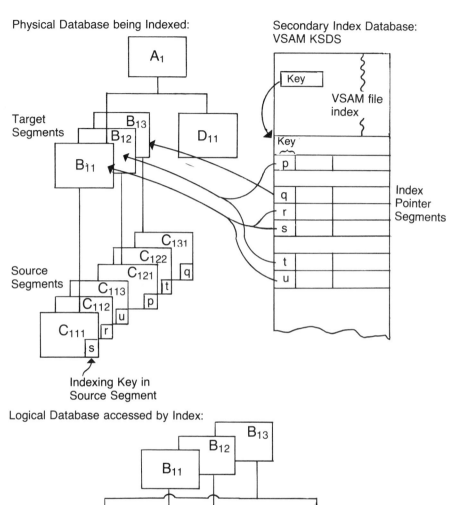

Figure 60   DL/1 Secondary Indexing

Secondary indexing uses a Secondary Index Database, which is implemented as a VSAM KSDS, containing Index Pointer Segments. Figure 60 shows how a secondary index works. The target segment may be viewed as the root segment of a logical database record having its own dependents and its parent, grandparent, etc, as dependents.

TOTAL

TOTAL requires one or more operating system data sets, each one corresponding to a TOTAL Master Data Set or a Variable Entry Data Set, and an optional log tape (Figure 61). TOTAL uses the operating system's direct-access method for accessing the data sets.

MASTER DATA SETS

A Master Data Set consists of fixed-length physical blocks of data which can hold one or more fixed-length logical database records. Each logical record has a control field which may be one field in the record or the concatenation of a number of fields. This control field or logical key is used by the direct-access method to store and retrieve the record.

Each control field within a given Master Data Set must be unique. When a record is added to a Master Data Set, TOTAL verifies that it is unique. If an attempt is made to add a record with a duplicate control field TOTAL informs the programmer of the error through a response code.

The control field is processed by a hashing algorithm to determine its preferred storage location within the direct-access file. If the preferred location already contains a record the new record is stored as close to this preferred location as possible, usually in the same physical block. If the physical block is full TOTAL will try to place the record on the same track or cylinder until an available location is found.

Records which hash to the same preferred location are called 'synonyms'. Those records that cannot be stored in the preferred location are linked to this location by a synonym chain. When retrieving a record, TOTAL reads the records in the synonym chain until the record with the required control field is found.

TOTAL always attempts to eliminate or shorten its synonym chains. If a synonym record is stored in the preferred location of a record which is to be added to the database, the system moves the synonym record to another free location so that the new record can be stored in its proper

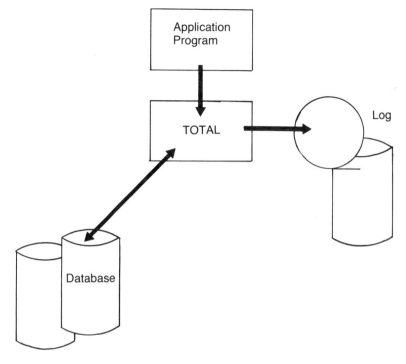

Figure 61   TOTAL Files

place. When a record which was stored in its preferred location is deleted and a synonym chain exists, TOTAL replaces the deleted record with the last record in the chain. This will tend to reduce the number of physical blocks containing the chain.

A Master record has a prefix called the ROOT field (Figure 62). This is used by the system to manage the synonym chain. The next field in the record is the control key. This is followed by the data elements and items. One pair of pointers, one next and one prior, is maintained for each LINKPATH in which the record participates. These LINKPATHs may be defined in any position following the control key.

VARIABLE ENTRY DATA SETS
A Variable Entry Data Set consists of fixed-length logical records which are usually 'blocked'. Although TOTAL only reads and writes fixed-

Master Data Set Record:
Root
Key
Data
. . . .
Data Elements and Items
Pairs of Pointers for each LINKPATH
Variable Entry Data Set Record:
Key1
Key2
. . . .
Data
Link1
Link2
. . . .
Control Fields of Master Records to which the Record is linked
Data Elements and Items
One pair of pointers for each LINKPATH

Figure 62 TOTAL Record Structure

Master Data Set
Variable Entry Data Set
EXAM
Data
PLES
Data
EXAM
Data
EXAM
Data
EXAM
Data
PLES
Data
PLES
Data

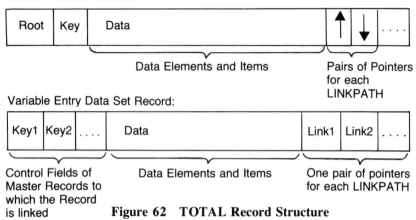

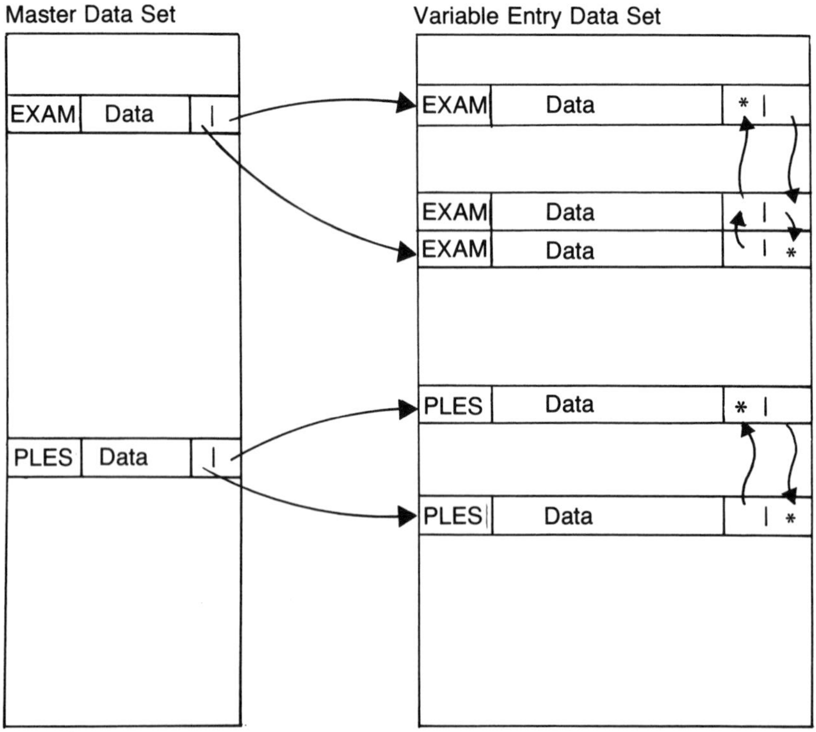

Figure 63 TOTAL LINKPATH Example

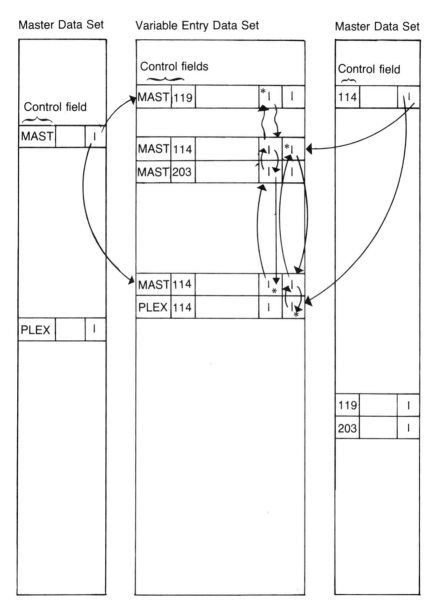

Figure 64 TOTAL (One Variable and Many Master Data Sets)

length records the Data Set may contain a number of different record types which have different record lengths. In this case the logical record length for the Data Set will equal the length of the longest record type. Shorter record types will contain unused space at the end.

Records in a Variable Entry Data Set are accessed via a record in a Master Data Set. A number of records in a Variable Entry Data Set are linked to one Master Data Set record by next and prior pointers to form a chain which is called a LINKPATH as illustrated in Figure 63. The pointers are the relative record direct-access addresses of the records in the Variable Entry Data Set. Each record in the Variable Entry Data Set holds the control key of the Master record which owns it.

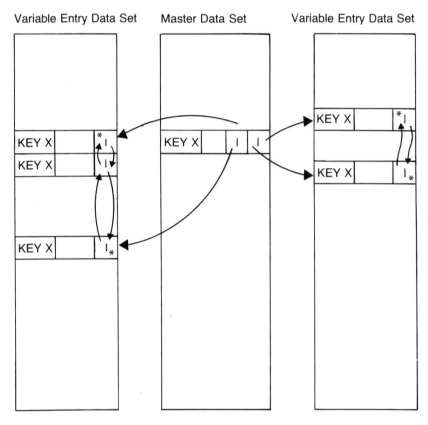

Figure 65   TOTAL (One Master and Many Variable Data Sets)

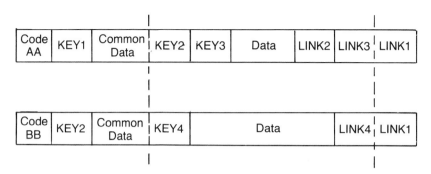

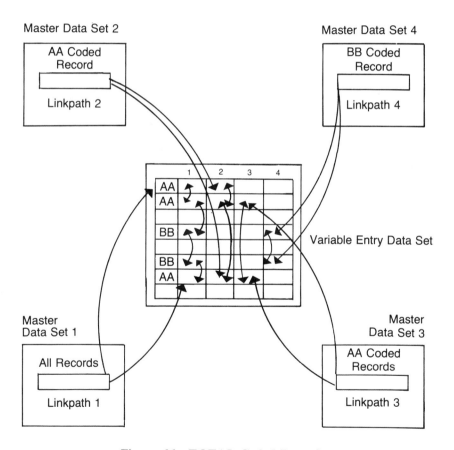

Figure 66   TOTAL Coded Records

A Variable Entry Data Set may have linkages from one, or more, Master Data Sets as illustrated in Figure 64. One or more Variable Entry Data Sets may have linkages from one Master Data Set as shown in Figure 65.

A Variable Entry record contains the Control Fields of all the Master records linked to it by LINKPATHs, one pair of linkage fields for each LINKPATH associated with it and as many data elements and items as required (Figure 62). These may be defined in any sequence, provided that each control field is defined in the record prior to its associated LINKPATH. If the Variable Entry Data Set is to contain a number of different record types a 'Coded Record' facility can be used. The physical format of Coded Records depends upon the number of LINKPATHs that each particular type participates in. The two records illustrated in Figure 66 are linked to the same Master Data Set via KEY1. The record with code 'AA' has linkages to two additional Master Data Sets via KEY2 and KEY3. The record with code 'BB' is linked to a fourth Master Data Set.

A control record at the start of each cylinder of the Variable Entry Data Set keeps a record of the free space in that cylinder. This information is used to monitor the 'LOAD LIMIT'. A field in the control record points to the next free location in the cylinder. The system attempts to place all the records on a primary LINKPATH in the same cylinder or range of cylinders.

ACCESSING THE DATA

The purpose of this section is to summarise, for each of the five DBMSs, the different ways in which the data on a database may be accessed. Appropriate data manipulation commands are provided by each DBMS to support the access techniques that are provided. The descriptions also indicate whether it would be possible to access the data without using the DBMS.

ADABAS

ADABAS commands allow a file to be read serially (physically sequentially), logically sequentially, in chronological sequence or randomly. When a file is read serially the Association Network and the Address Converter are not used. Records are read in the physical sequence that they appear on the file, either starting from the front of file or from a specified record.

When a file or part of a file is read logically sequentially the Association Network and the Address Converter are used. The inverted list for a descriptor, maintained in ascending value sequence and ISN sequence for each value, is accessed in ascending value (logical) sequence and records retrieved. Logical sequential access can start at the lowest value in the inverted list or from a specific value.

If records are to be retrieved in chronological sequence, ie in the sequence in which they appeared on file, then the records are retrieved in ISN order by serially reading the Address Converter.

ADABAS also supports a Histogram command which retrieves from the Association Network for a specified descriptor the number of times each value of the descriptor occurs on file in ascending sequence of descriptor values.

Records can be accessed randomly by descriptor value or by ISN. Complex enquiries are serviced in one ADABAS call by connecting up to 125 different descriptors by the use of Boolean logic. This includes range values, 'BUT NOT' and sorting. Resolution of such complex searches to produce target ISNs is performed in the Association Network.

Up to 250 files can be held in an ADABAS database and these files can be related by common values being designated as descriptors. For example, if the customer file is being accessed, the orders relating to that customer can be retrieved from the Orders file by accessing the customer number which is a descriptor on the Orders file. In this way navigation is possible across a whole network of files in any direction.

ADABAS also has an access method, called the ADABAS Direct Access Method or ADAM, which is based on hashing techniques. One descriptor per file, which must be unique, may be specified as an ADAM Key. Access is achieved by hashing the descriptor value onto a 'home' block so only one I/O per access is usually required.

If overflow of the 'home' block occurs, ADABAS will place the record in Data Storage using the Free Space Management Tables held in the Associator. Index entries are maintained for ADAM keys so that if a record is not found in its 'home' block, ADABAS reverts to its normal access method. An installation can determine the degree of record scatter/overflow by fixing the hashing length of the key field. A utility ADAMER – the Adam Estimation Routine – is available to assist in calculating the optimum hash length and space requirements.

All the access techniques address the data at the field or group level. The programmer, or ADAMINT interface, identifies the data units to be transferred to the program by their names.

ADABAS files store the data in a compressed format and they could consist of up to five sections of Data Storage if secondary space allocation has been invoked, so it would be difficult to read the file without using ADABAS. A utility is provided which unloads a database file into its uncompressed standard format so that it may be accessed by non-database programs.

DMS 1100

DMS 1100 provides facilities for accessing data serially (physically sequentially), sequentially and randomly. A database area, containing data but not indexes or pointer arrays, may be read serially. An area may be read forward or backwards from a specified starting position. The programmer may choose to accept records of any type (an area usually contains a number of record types) or just those of a specified type.

Sequential access can be achieved by use of the INDEX SEQUEN-TIAL record location mode. The records may then be accessed in ascending or descending key sequence. A set with a mode of POINTER ARRAY can also be accessed sequentially. Records may also be accessed sequentially by reading round a chained set which may be ordered in first-in first-out, last-in first-out or sorted into ascending/descending sequence.

Records with a location mode of 'CALC' can be accessed randomly by use of the CALC key. This key is hashed to produce the record's target page and calc chain. This page is then read and the appropriate calc chain searched for a record of the correct type having the required Key field. Duplicate Keys can be allowed or disallowed; retrieval commands are provided to deal with duplicates.

Database keys may be used to access records directly. A database key consists of the concatenation of an area code, a page number within an area and a record number within the page. The system accesses the required page directly and locates the required record within the page using the record number.

The ACQUIRE command, which is not in the CODASYL recommendations, retrieves all or a specified number of database keys from the current occurrence of a pointer array set. These database keys may then be used to access the record directly. The programmer can, through application program coding, logically compare two or more lists of database keys in order to select records for retrieval.

The access techniques available under DMS 1100 address data at the record level. The record layout used by an application system can be a subset of the physical record. The mapping from the physical record to the logical record (program view) is handled by the subschema.

IDMS

IDMS commands allow data to be accessed serially (physically sequentially), sequentially, by generic key, and randomly. Any database AREA may be read serially, either forward or backwards from a specified starting position. The programmer may choose to accept records of any type or alternatively select only those of a specified record type. (An AREA will usually contain a number of record types.)

Sequential access can be achieved by the use of the indexing facility. An index of sorted record keys is used to process the records sequentially. The use of an index key has allowed a generic key facility to be provided. It is possible to access all the records which have the same partial key. Records may also be accessed sequentially by reading round a set of member records which may be maintained in first-in first-out, last-in first-out or sorted into ascending/descending sequence.

Any record with a storage mode of 'CALC' can be accessed randomly by use of its CALC key. This key is hashed to produce the record's target page. This page is then read and its system calc chain is searched for a record of the correct type having the required key field. Records with a storage mode of 'CALC' can optionally be allowed to have duplicate keys and retrieval commands are provided to access these.

Records may be accessed directly if their database keys are known. In this case the system reads the appropriate page and references the line index entry to locate the record within the page. The database key consists of the page number concatenated with the line index number.

All of the access techniques available under IDMS address the data at the record level. The record formats used by an application system can be a subset of the physical record. The mapping from the physical record to the logical record is performed by the subschema. The subschema used by a program also defines which records, sets and areas may be used.

IDMS's data sets or Files are direct access files containing Pages. The format of a database Page is not simple, so it would be difficult to read the data directly without using IDMS.

IMS-DL/1

This section describes how the data may be accessed in general terms. SHSAM and HSAM only allow serial access to the data from the start of the physical database (file). HDAM allows access either from the start of the physical database (file) or from a specified starting position.

The indexed access methods provide sequential access to root segments in ascending key sequence. Processing may begin at the lowest key or from a specified starting position. Secondary indexes may be used to access a segment in an order specified by a key constructed from fields in the segment or one of its dependents. Dependent segments of a given type which have a sequence field (key) are ordered sequentially by their sequence field under their parent.

SHISAM, HISAM, HDAM and HIDAM allow root segments to be retrieved randomly by specifying their key. The indexed access methods use an index look-up technique to retrieve the requested record. HDAM uses a key hashing technique.

SHSAM and HSAM only allow retrieval after the initial loading. All the other access methods support retrieval and update, ie insert, delete and replace.

Internally DL/1 uses physical addresses as pointers. However, addressing at this level is not available to the programmer.

All of these access methods allow the programmer to address the data at the segment level by name. DL/1 moves the segment, or path of segments, to and from the program's I/O area. The Field Level Sensitivity feature allows an ordered list of segment fields to be addressed.

SHSAM, HSAM, SHISAM and HISAM physical database (files) have a relatively simple structure so they could be accessed by a user written program without using the DL/1 software. HDAM and HIDAM use internal pointers and have a complex physical organisation, so access by a user written program without the aid of DL/1 would be difficult.

TOTAL

TOTAL commands are available for accessing the data serially (physically sequentially), sequentially and randomly. Both Master and Variable Entry Data Sets may be read serially, either from the beginning of the Data Set or from a specified starting point.

Sequential access is achieved by reading the records on a given LINK-PATH. Entry to a given Linkpath is gained either by first accessing an appropriate Master record and following the pointers or by serially searching the Data Set for records that are heads of chains for that Linkpath. Records on a Linkpath may be read forwards or backwards. The sequential order of the records is determined by the way in which the user stores the records since they may be added to or deleted from any point in the chain.

Master Data Sets are normally accessed randomly. There are no facilities for reading them sequentially. The control field (logical key) of the required record is processed by a hashing algorithm to produce the preferred 'relative record' location where the record may be stored. This record is read and its control key is checked. If it is not the required record the system searches down a synonym chain until the requested record is found. If the requested record is not found the requestor is informed that the record is not in the Data Set.

Variable Entry Data Sets and Master Data Sets can be accessed directly if the 'relative record' addresses of the records of interest are known. This information can be obtained from previous TOTAL requests. Notice however, that the relative record address of a record may be changed by the system, if for example a synonym record is relocated.

All of these access methods allow the programmer to address the data at the data-item (field) or element/subelement (group) level. The programmer identifies them by specifying their names. TOTAL extracts the required data from the database record and moves it into the program's data area.

TOTAL's Data Sets are direct access files containing fixed length records. The record format is simple since multiple fields, repeating groups and data compression are not supported. It would therefore be possible to read the Data Sets without using the TOTAL software.

BUFFERING TECHNIQUES

This section briefly describes the buffering techniques used by the five DBMSs. The descriptions explain how the buffer sizes are determined and indicate whether a number of buffer pools may be allocated. The algorithms for re-using buffers are also discussed.

The buffering mechanism determines how data is transferred from secondary storage (usually disk) into the computer's memory. A buffer is an area in the computer's memory, which is allocated by the DBMS, used to hold a physical block of data which has been read from a database file. Data is transferred between the working storage of application programs and the buffer by the DBMS. The collective term for a number of buffers is a buffer pool. Some DBMSs allow a number of buffer pools to be allocated, each buffer pool being used for one or more specific record types.

The size of the buffers, number of buffers, buffer pooling arrangements and buffer selection algorithm are factors which can have a dramatic effect on the performance of the DBMS. Performance is discussed in Chapter 6.

ADABAS

ADABAS uses one buffer pool for the database and the Associator. In the multiuser environment this buffer pool is shared by all active programs. The blocksize of the Associator is half that of Data Storage. These blocksizes are normally determined by the system although they may be changed.

A buffer pool management algorithm is used to determine which buffer is to be used for a read request. This algorithm counts the number of read references and the number of update references for each buffer. It also uses an ADABAS transaction counter to indicate when the buffer was last used.

If a suitable buffer cannot be found, either because buffers have been updated and cannot be overwritten, or because some buffers are currently being referenced very frequently, then ADABAS will write all updated buffers back to the database. *All* buffers which have been updated are written to the database by issuing one operating system write command per physical device. The buffers are written in ascending order, ie cylinder-head sequence, for efficiency. The update counts are then reset to zero so the buffering algorithm will then be able to select a suitable buffer.

DMS 1100

DMS 1100 uses a central buffer pool. Its size is specified at system generation time and cannot be altered dynamically. This buffer area is shared by pages from data, index and pointer areas. Buffers are selected for reuse by using the 'Least Recently Used' algorithm. If the selected buffer has been updated it is written back to the database.

IDMS

When IDMS is run in the local, or single user mode, each user has one or more private buffer pools. The Central Version of IDMS, however, has one or more buffer pools which are shared by all the run-units (programs) under its control. The buffer pool is defined using the Device Media Control Language or Service Description Language.

For each buffer pool defined, it is necessary to specify how many pages of a given size it is to hold. Each Area defined is then allocated to one of these buffer pools. A number of Areas may share a buffer pool but if the page sizes for these areas differ the buffer pool must be defined to hold the largest page size. Areas cannot be allocated to more than one buffer pool.

The buffering algorithm selects the least frequently used buffer for reuse. Pages which have been updated are written back to the database. Buffers which have not been updated are simply overwritten.

In the ICL implementation each IDMS run-unit has a private buffer pool, irrespective of whether an unshared or shared service is being used. Under a shared service any number of run-units may have a copy of a given page in their private buffer pool if they are only accessing it. If a run-unit wishes to update that page the system will apply a page lock. Only one run-unit may update lock a page so concurrent updating of different copies of a given page cannot occur. The number of buffers to be used is defined in the Service Description, although this can be altered at run time.

IMS-DL/1

DL/1 allows between 1 and 255 buffer subpools to be defined. For each buffer subpool it is possible to specify the number of buffers to be allocated, the DBDs which are to use the buffer pool and the buffer requirements for any associated indexes. Under the VSAM access method the size of a buffer within a subpool is determined by the largest VSAM control interval size (blocksize) used. Buffers within a subpool are reused on a 'last used longest ago' basis.

TOTAL

The buffering requirements are specified using the Data Base Definition Language which is used to produce the 'DBMOD'. The number of buffers to be allocated to each file can be specified, the default being one. The size of the buffers is determined by the blocksizes of the files.

It is also possible to allow a number of files to share a buffer pool. A number of Master Data Sets or a number of Variable Entry Data Sets may share a buffer pool, but a mixture of the two types of file is not allowed. If the blocksizes of the files sharing a buffer pool vary the buffer size is determined by the largest blocksize.

Reuse of the buffers within a pool is based on a simple ageing algorithm. When a new block of data needs to be read the buffer which has not been referenced for the longest time is overwritten, after being rewritten to the database if it has been updated.

6 Installation and Operation

The objectives of this chapter are to:

— discuss, in general terms, some of the facilities required in a DBMS to manage the day to day and longer term operational problems;

and for each of the five DBMSs to:

— briefly comment on the system generation procedures;

— describe how a database is physically established on the computer;

— identify the major aids provided to support the DBMS;

— describe how the database can be changed to accommodate larger volumes of data and new data structures;

— identify the facilities provided which can be used to monitor and tune the database system;

— discuss the optimisation of secondary storage;

— consider the optimisation of access times.

INTRODUCTION

The previous chapters of this book explain how five different DBMSs function and how they interface with application programs and their host operating system. This chapter considers how they are put onto the computer in the first instance and what facilities are provided to maintain an operational database. Before an application program can access a database three preparatory processes must be performed by either the vendor or the user.

— Installation of the Software

Installation involves establishing current copies of the DBMS component modules in the appropriate libraries on the computer.

— System Generation

The DBMS is tailored to meet the installation's requirements. Tailoring involves specifying which facilities of the DBMS are to be used. These facilities, or options, are specified by means of parameters. Such parameters are usually termed system generation parameters. The extent to which a DBMS can be tailored varies from DBMS to DBMS.

— Creation of the Database

Before a database can be physically created a lot of work must be performed to decide what data should be held and how it should be structured to model the organisation's data. A discussion of database design is beyond the scope of the present work but a readable introductory account may be found in items 6, 7 and 8, especially 7 in the bibliography. First, the required data structures and the relationships between them are described by means of the Data Definition facilities described in Chapter 4. Then the physical databases may be created. Database creation involves the allocation and formatting of the operating system files which are to hold the database. Application programs may then be run to add data to the initially empty database. Alternatively, if the data is already available, a load utility program provided with the DBMS may be used to establish the database, or part of it.

When the DBMS has been installed, the system generated and the database created, application programs may be developed. In order to support the development, testing and live execution of database application programs the DBMS needs to provide operational aids to:

— Identify Errors

The DBMS and its supporting utilities must provide appropriate messages or response codes if an error or unusual condition is detected. Supporting documentation should adequately explain what kind of problems can cause each message or code to be generated. The precision with which an error code identifies the cause of a problem can dramatically affect the time it takes to 'debug' a program thereby increasing programmer productivity or reducing the down time of a live program.

— Test New Programs

A production database should not be used for testing, especially if the program performs updates, because there is a danger that the live data may be corrupted. In addition, the production database is likely to contain large volumes of data which would result in excessive run times for test jobs. It is usually necessary to support a testing database.

— Supply Accounting Information

Some installations consider the DBMS machine time and input/output to be an operational overhead. Others may choose to charge the resources used by the DBMS to those programs which used them. In order to allow this to be done the DBMS must be capable of supplying the appropriate statistics. An exact and repeatable apportionment of costs is not always possible. For example, a shared buffer pool may result in contention between two concurrently executing programs, one program's request may cause a buffer read for the other program to be flushed.

It is very unlikely that the database will remain unchanged after it has been initially created and loaded. The volume of data held on the database will probably increase and new application systems are likely to require new data structures to be added or existing ones to be modified. Consequently, a DBMS must provide facilities for maintaining the database. Such maintenance falls into two categories:

— Reorganisation

Reorganisation involves changing the physical organisation of the database without changing the logical view. The physical organisation may need to be changed for a number of reasons. It may be necessary if the database is filled to capacity or if performance has degraded.

— Restructuring

Restructuring involves changing the logical structure of the database. The logical structure may need to be changed in order to add new record types and relationships needed to support new application systems.

The performance of the DBMS, the physical database and the application systems using them is of great interest, possibly concern, to the DBMS users. The performance of the DBMS code itself is under the control of its vendor although performance may be influenced by a wise choice of system generation options. Application system performance is dependent upon two major factors. Firstly, the general programming skills of the programmers and, more specifically, their knowledge of the data manipulation facilities which allows them to select the most efficient means of accessing the data. Secondly, the general performance of the physical database strongly influences the performance of application systems.

Database Design has a major bearing on the performance of a database system. A discussion of this is beyond the scope of the present work but item 7 in the bibliography provides a good readable discussion. In this book we are concerned with the facilities offered by a DBMS to allow the database system to be monitored so its use of storage and machine time can be optimised.

Performance is really in the eye of the beholder. Ideally an installation would like to have a DBMS that used no machine time, no main memory and no secondary storage. In practice tuning involves a compromise between these three resources. It is therefore essential that there are clear objectives when undertaking a tuning exercise.

Consider, for example, a situation where it is necessary to minimise the main memory occupation of a DBMS. The number of buffers will have to be reduced to a minimum. This will probably cause excessive buffer flushing thereby increasing the machine time and input/output activity. The size of these buffers could also be reduced thus increasing the machine time and I/O activity. Smaller buffers imply smaller blocks which may result in less efficient space management, thereby causing secondary storage requirements to rise.

INSTALLATION AND SYSTEM GENERATION

This section briefly comments on the installation procedure for each of the five DBMSs. Installation and system generation are not only performed when the DBMS is first installed. It will be necessary to reinstall and regenerate the system whenever new versions of the software are released. New versions are usually produced to either correct serious errors or provide new facilities. Regeneration of the software may also be performed to change the system generation options should the requirements change.

ADABAS

The ADABAS software is distributed on a magnetic tape which contains the programs in relocatable object module format. Installation of the software involves cataloguing the object modules to a suitable library and link editing the ADABAS nucleus and the utilities. A utility is available which will generate a complete installation job stream. Initial installation is performed by the vendor.

If ADABAS is to be used in the multiuser mode a new supervisor call has to be added to the operating system. The supervisor call is used for communication between the multiuser version of ADABAS and application programs running in other regions or partitions.

The actual generation of the ADABAS system only requires a dozen cards which specify such things as:

— the sizes of the Data Storage and Associator;

— the installation tape number;

— the environment:– single user or multiuser mode;

— the logging options to be used.

It is also possible to override the default blocksizes for the database data sets. However, users are recommended to use the default blocksizes which have been calculated to give optimum performance.

DMS 1100

The DMS 1100 software is distributed on a multiple magnetic tape. One of the files on the tape contains a run stream which will generate a new version of DMS 1100. System generation statements are input to this run stream. These statements specify:

— whether a Single Threading or a Multi Threading version is to be created;

— which components of DMS 1100 are to be generated.

The schema and subschema compilers use a DMS 1100 database internally. In order to create their database during the system generation, the installation tape contains a default version of the software and a default schema and subschema for the compilers.

The Data Management Routine uses a System File to record information about the database. After the system has been installed this file is allocated and initialised by a utility. Once it has been initialised it should not be reinitialised. Its integrity is maintained by the recovery facilities.

IDMS

The IDMS software is supplied on a magnetic tape. This tape contains a number of files, each one being a specific part of the system. An installation utility is provided on the first file of the tape which reads a few installation option cards and then generates an installation job stream by selecting the required components from the tape. The installation option cards are used to identify which libraries are to be used, the name, location and size of the directory to be created and the name and location of the files which are created to run a test job stream.

The installation job stream is then run. This will catalogue the required object material, source macros and sample schema and program to the selected libraries. The sample schema is generated and a sample test job is executed. If the software is to run in local mode the installation is complete.

In order to run the central version of IDMS it is necessary to perform a Central Version Generation and add a communication supervisor call (SVC) to the operating system. The 'CVGEN' involves specifying a number of macros. The simplest CVGEN consists of two macros with three Parameters. The other optional macros provide tools for controlling and tuning the system. It is interesting to note that the central version of IDMS is also the nucleus of Cullinane's teleprocessing monitor IDMS-DC. The vendor will usually install and generate the software.

The ICL versions of IDMS are normally installed by ICL's technical staff. The software is supplied on a magnetic tape. The code and execution macros (equivalent to JCL procedures) are loaded into the appropriate libraries. Execution macros are provided for starting a 'service' and for running all of the utilities.

IMS-DL/1

IMS/VS and DOS/VS DL/1 software can be distributed on either disk or tape. The distribution material consists of a number of source, object (relocatable) and load (core image) libraries. The source libraries contain DL/1 system macros and DL/1 source code. The object and load libaries contain IBM generated versions of the DL/1 modules; IBM call such a system a 'Starter System'.

The software may be tailored to the user's installation by performing a System Generation. This involves specifying a number of parameters on system generation macros to define the required operating environment, such as the logging requirements, buffering options and maximum number of multi-tasked users. Alternatively, the System Installation Productivity Option provides a pre-generated default system.

TOTAL

The TOTAL software is distributed on a magnetic tape which contains the programs in relocatable object module format. Installation of the software involves cataloguing the object modules and utilities to suitable libraries and generating option modules to tailor the system. If the central version of TOTAL is to be used a special inter-region communication SVC must be added to the operating system.

The TOTAL control program is then link edited. A macro expansion generates the linkage editor control statements needed to catalogue the required modules. These modules will only support the optional features requested in the generation options. Finally, the database files need to be formatted and the required system files allocated.

CREATING THE DATABASE

The following descriptions explain how a database which may be accessed by application programs is created. It is assumed that the database has been designed. The first step which must be taken to create a physical database is the specification of the requirements. This is done by defining the data to the system by means of the Data Definition facilities described in Chapter 4. This section assumes that the data has already been defined, as described in Chapter 4, and that the description is available to the creation programs in the form of the ASSOCIATOR, SCHEMA, DMCL/SDL, DBD and DBMOD respectively for the five systems.

Database creation involves allocating the physical files described in the data definition. Once allocated these files are usually formatted by a utility. Formatting involves writing blocks to the files which include space management information indicating that the block contains no records. The empty database may then be loaded by user written application programs or by a load utility if one is provided.

ADABAS

Database creation begins with the allocation and formatting of the operating system data sets which comprise the database. Once this has been done individual ADABAS files may be created. This involves three distinct phases.

In the first phase the DDL, which is used to define the attributes of the fields within the file to be loaded, is analysed. The raw data is also edited and compressed by the load utility. This utility has a user exit which may be used to perform special data editing. It also ensures that the data format is consistent with the field attributes. The processed data is written out to an operating system data set, usually a tape, in the compressed format used by ADABAS.

The second phase stores the information obtained from the DDL in the Associator. The edited and compressed data is also loaded into Data Storage by this phase of the load utility. At this stage the maximum size of the file and how much free space should be left in the Associator and Data Storage part of the file to cater for future update activity are specified. As the data is loaded the descriptor values are extracted for use in the third phase.

The third phase generates the inverted lists and stores them in the Associator. If the file contains multiple descriptors all the inverted lists are generated in one run of the utility.

DMS 1100

The Schema contains the specifications of the Areas of the database which correspond to operating system files. A 'Data Management Utility' is used to initialise the Areas of the database. Alternatively, an area may be initialised automatically by DMS 1100 when it is opened for INITIAL LOAD. Once the database has been initialised, with empty pages, application programs may be written to load the data.

IDMS

The control block produced by compiling the Device Media Control or Service Description Language contains a full description of the physical characteristics of the files and their logical subdivision. The required size of the operating system data sets is calculated from the page size and number of pages per file. A format utility is then run to pre-format the database files with empty pages.

Before the Schema, DMCL and Subschema compilers can be run a Data Directory must be created. The Data Directory is itself an IDMS database which must be created! A macro is provided for its creation in order to allow the compilers to be executed.

After the database has been formatted data may be loaded in two ways. Application programs may be written to load the data as a standard part of an application system. Alternatively, if it is necessary to load a large volume of existing data, a load utility may be used. This utility is controlled by a user written exit which reads, formats and checks the data before passing it to the utility for loading.

IMS-DL/1

The database is defined by the physical DBDs which describe the physical databases (files) which comprise the database. The output from the DBD Generation includes the VSAM Access Method Services control commands needed to define the required VSAM data sets. Before application programs can access the database one or more PSBs must be defined. User programs must be written to load the database.

If the 'load' option is used by the program a root segment's dependents must be inserted in their correct hierarchical sequence. SHSAM and HSAM physical databases must be loaded in the required processing sequence. SHISAM, HISAM and HIDAM must be loaded in ascending sequence field (Key) order. HDAM allows loading in any physical database record sequence. If the database being loaded includes logical relationships or secondary indexes a number of utilities must be run in order to resolve the various pointers.

TOTAL

The first step in the creation of a TOTAL database is the definition of the data. This is done using the Data Base Definition Language (DBDL) which describes the logical and physical characteristics of each TOTAL data set together with the relationships between them. The DBMOD is generated from the DBDL statements which is a machine loadable module describing a database view.

The second step uses the 'DBMOD' to format the TOTAL data sets. One operating system data set is allocated for each and every TOTAL data set. A FORMAT utility is used to initialise these data sets. Initialisation involves formatting the physical blocks with empty logical records.

After the data sets have been formatted the database may be loaded. Application programs may be written to perform the load. Alternatively, a load utility provided may be used. In order to use this utility it is necessary to put the data into the required format and specify a few control parameters. The load utility is designed to load large volumes of data efficiently.

OPERATIONAL AIDS

The facilities provided by the five DBMSs which aid the operational use of the system are considered in this section. In particular it considers how errors are indicated and what aids are provided for testing application programs. It also considers how the DBMS machine overheads may be allocated to application programs for charging purposes.

ADABAS

The ADABAS nucleus provides the programmer and DBA with diagnostic response codes if an error condition is detected. A manual is provided which documents the possible reasons why each response code has been generated. This information assists in the detection and correction of errors in database programs. The utilities produce self explanatory messages if an error is detected.

Database programs which are under development can be tested using a second ADABAS nucleus against a test database. The ease with which ADABAS files may be created makes this a practical option. Alternatively a group of files within the production database may be designated as test files. If it is necessary to test against a live database it is possible to tell ADABAS to accept, but ignore, all update commands. If ADAMINT is being used the interface can be programmed to use test files during development and maintenance.

ADABAS can optionally produce statistics which include details of all ADABAS requests and input/output activity. These statistics can therefore be used to monitor and tune the system. They may also be used for accounting purposes. ADABAS records the program name, start and finish time and I/O details associated with each request. It would therefore be possible to charge back the overheads of running the database system to the program using it.

DMS 1100

The Data Management Routine returns a diagnostic response code to the programmer if an error condition is detected. A manual documents the causes of each response code. This information assists in the detection and correction of errors in database programs.

Programs may be tested in the Test or Training mode. The Test mode accepts update requests and maintains a change file but does not update the database. In Test/Training mode DMS 1100 uses test Areas for programs being tested and maintains a change file. In the Training mode production programs run against training areas.

Facilities are provided for the collection of statistics which can be used to monitor the performance of the system as a whole. Individual programs may also request DMS 1100 to return statistics in the program's communications block. These statistics give command counts and queueing statistics for that program's execution.

The DMS 1100 code is executed as if it were a subroutine to the application program. Central Processor Unit time and Input/Output will therefore be automatically charged to the application by the standard operating system accounting routines.

IDMS

IDMS returns a response code to the programmer to indicate how a command has been processed. The response codes are documented, with possible causes, thus helping the programmer to resolve errors. Application programmers may also use a DEBUG option which causes the DML sequence number, which is printed on the compiled program listing, of a failing command together with other status information to be displayed. A utility allows selected parts, or all, of the database to be printed in hexadecimal and character formats with interpreted database keys.

There are currently no accounting aids which allow the Central Version services to be charged out to individual run-units. User written procedures could be used to accept the IDMS statistics for this purpose.

The ICL version allows a TRACE to be started to output details of all the DML commands executed to the job log. IDMS is executed as if it were the subroutine of the application program. Control is not relinquished to another virtual machine to service the database request. The IDMS service will therefore be charged out to the virtual machines using it by the standard operating system accounting facility.

IMS-DL/1

DL/1 returns a status code to the programmer after each CALL. This status code indicates whether the previous request was successfully completed. These codes and their documented meanings help the programmer to detect and correct errors in programs. A DL/1 CALL simulator is available which can be used to test programs.

IMS/VS has a monitoring facility which allows statistical information to be collected. A utility can produce a number of reports from the collected statistics such as Buffer Pool usage, Program I/O and DL/1 Call Summary. VSAM's Access Method Service utility can be used to report the status of the VSAM data sets.

TOTAL

TOTAL provides the programmer with diagnostic response codes if an error condition is detected. The documentation lists possible causes of each response code. This information is therefore valuable for the detection and correction of errors in database programs. The utilities produce self explanatory messages if an error is detected.

Database programs which are being developed or maintained could be tested against a test database. If the test database is smaller than the live one it would be necessary to generate a suitably tailored 'DBMOD' either under a different name or under the same name and stored in a test library. TOTAL does not provide any special features to overcome this testing problem.

The TOTAL utilities include a database Print/Modify program. The Print function allows selected parts of TOTAL files to be printed in both character and hexadecimal format. The Modify function allows fields within selected records to be conditionally replaced with new data.

TOTAL can optionally collect run-time statistical data. A utility is provided to print the statistics file. Application programs may also use a special TOTAL DML command to read the statistics file. Explicit accounting data is not provided. However the run-time statistics and possibly the log information could be used for accounting purposes.

DATABASE RESTRUCTURING AND REORGANISATION

This section describes the facilities provided by the five DBMSs for restructuring and reorganising a database. These facilities allow the database to be expanded and changed as conditions within the organisation alter.

ADABAS

Changes to the logical structures of an ADABAS database can be made without having to reorganise it. Such changes as creating new files, adding fields to an existing record or creating new descriptors can be performed by utilities or through the Data Dictionary System.

The space utilisation may be monitored by running a utility which documents the free space in Data Storage. A file reorganisation will pull together any fragmented extents. However, because of the indexing structure, fragmented extents will have a minimal effect on performance. New physical extents can be added to Data Storage without reorganising the whole database.

Degrading access times can be detected by studying run statistics that ADABAS produces. Degradation can result from a large number of records being added to a file which is accessed sequentially. The physical sequence will gradually diverge from the logical sequence. If the file is read sequentially this will result in a gradually increasing I/O overhead. Reorganisation in this case involves reordering the Data Storage element of the file in order to optimise logical sequential access. In this case only the Address Converter is affected, the index structure is unchanged.

Reorganisation or reordering of an ADABAS file is achieved by simply unloading it, changing size parameters if necessary, and then reloading it using supplied utilities. It may not be necessary to reorganise the whole database, any particular file may be reorganised without affecting other files. When a file is reorganised the ISNs of the records are not changed so the system only has to update the Address Converter when the data is reloaded.

The Associator may also be reorganised by using a utility. The index structure could become fragmented if records are added causing it to split, and subsequently records are deleted leaving a lot of free space in the index blocks.

DMS 1100

A Data Reorganisation Utility is provided with DMS 1100 which performs physical reorganisation and logical restructuring of the database. The utility is driven by a Reorganisation Control Language which is used to explicitly specify which areas, records and sets are to be reorganised. The utility examines the schema to determine whether other parts of the database will be affected by the requested reorganisation, for example other areas containing records with pointers to a record type which is being reorganised, and if necessary implicitly causes them to be unloaded.

Logical structuring facilities which are planned will allow areas, record types and set relationships to be added, removed or changed. Fields may be added to or deleted from a record type and their attributes, ie size and format, may be altered. The characteristics of a set relationship may be changed, new relationships may be added or existing ones deleted. Restructuring enables the database to develop and change with the organisation whose data it contains. The consequences of restructuring on existing programs must be considered.

Physical reorganisation allows the physical, as distinct from the logical, structure of the database to be changed. The sizes of areas and/or pages may be altered to accommodate a change in the data volumes. Performances may be improved by rebuilding indexes, removing records from overflow or grouping via members about their respective owners. Physical reorganisations are completely transparent to application program logic.

The utility may either unload and reload a number of areas (possibly the complete database) or, where possible, only the affected record types from the affected areas. For example, if a large number of additions and deletions of a particular record type has caused overflow problems, only that record type needs to be reorganised. If the changes require a new schema the utility uses the old schema view for unloading and the new schema view for reloading the affected parts of the database.

The Data Management Utility also provides a means of expanding the page size in situ. The utility also produces reports on the physical state of the database, such as the free space available.

IDMS

An IDMS database may need to be reorganised to allocate more space to an Area or to change the existing database structure in some way. Two types of reorganisation are possible using IDMS utilities. The data can be reorganised in situ by a Restructuring utility or alternatively a portion of the database can be reorganised (ie unloaded and reloaded).

The Restructuring utility can be used to change the format of the data portion of a record type. It can also change the number of pointer fields in the record prefix thereby allowing relationships to be added or deleted. The utility scans the Area(s) affected by the change reading the records, reformatting the prefix and data portions as required and then rewriting the newly formatted records. It will resolve any new pointers which may be required as a result of the change.

If a full reorganisation is necessary, for example to increase the size of an Area, to change the page size or to make major changes to the database structure, then the Unload and Reload utilities would be used. When an Area of the database is reorganised any other Areas which are connected to it by set type relationships must also be reorganised. This is necessary because the database keys of the records will be changed by the full reorganisation.

Additional space can also be given to an Area by using a utility which expands the existing pages allocated to the Area. As the number of pages does not change, the database keys are unchanged, so the database structures are unaffected.

A utility is available which provides a number of reports on selected Areas of the database. These reports include details of the amount and distribution of free space within an area and counts of the different record types in each area. A utility is also provided for tidying up the record indexes. The utility consolidates indexes, removing surplus index blocks and levels in an index hierarchy where possible.

IMS-DL/1

Reorganisation of a DL/1 database may be necessary in order to optimise the use of physical storage, to improve performance or to make logical changes to (restructure) physical database record types. Since SHSAM and HSAM physical databases (files) cannot be updated they will not need reorganising; they have to be recreated.

The other DL/1 access methods allow update to the VSAM data sets used to implement them. These may become inefficiently organised. The VSAM Access Method Services utility can be used to establish how full the data sets are and whether they need reorganising. HDAM and HIDAM will generally require less maintenance than HISAM as they reuse deleted space more efficiently. Under IMS a 'Database Surveyor' Utility is available which scans all or part of a HDAM or HIDAM database to determine the need for reorganisation.

The DL/1 execution statistics can be used to detect degrading performance. HDAM and HIDAM performance will gradually degrade as updating takes place. The physical sequence of the segments will diverge from the logical sequence. If new segments cannot be placed near their related segments this will increase the number of I/O operations needed to access the data. A reorganisation will optimise the placement of the segments. Reorganisation may also be used to change the physical attributes of the VSAM data set (eg physical block size, etc) in order to improve performance.

Restructuring of HDAM and HIDAM physical databases (files) is accomplished through the use of a Hierarchical Direct Unload utility. The physical database may be unloaded with a new DBD which defines the restructured physical database record type. New segment type paths may be added; existing unused ones may be deleted. However the hierarchical sequence of existing segment types must not be changed, ie a segment type cannot be deleted from or added into the middle of an existing path. The size of a segment type may be changed but it is the user's responsibility to reformat them; DL/1 simply truncates or pads the existing data as appropriate. The position and length of a sequence field (Key) cannot be changed.

TOTAL

Reorganisation of part of the database may be necessary if more space needs to be allocated to a Data Set to accommodate an increased volume of data or because performance has degraded. It may also be necessary if the structure of the database has to be changed, for example to add new fields or delete redundant ones.

Deteriorating performance can result for a number of reasons. A Master Data Set may be nearly full, or the hashing of the control fields may result in a clustering of the records in one part of the Data Set. In both cases long synonym chains may be generated. Searching of synonym chains when retrieving data and the maintenance of synonym chains resulting from additions and deletions will impose a gradually increasing overhead on the software. The system dynamically reorganises synonym chains so if the file has been allocated sufficient space and the control keys do not cause clustering, no reorganisation of Master Data Sets should be necessary.

Related Records in a Variable Entry Data Set can cause performance to degrade if they are not stored close to one another. This can result in excessive I/O and disk head seeking when reading all of the records on the primary LINKPATH.

A Master Data Set can easily be reorganised. It is only necessary to unload the Data Set, enlarge it and reload the data using utilities provided. When a Variable Entry Data Set is reorganised any Master Data Set related to it must have the pointers to the first and last records on the linkpath updated. A utility is provided to do this.

Restructuring is achieved by unloading the database, changing the database description and reloading. Fields may be added or deleted and new linkage paths defined, or old ones deleted.

MONITORING AND TUNING

The following descriptions summarise the facilities provided by each of the five DBMSs for monitoring the system so that it may be tuned. They indicate the kinds of statistical information available from the DBMS and what information about the state of the database can be obtained from utility programs. Facilities for optimising the use of secondary storage and minimising data access times are discussed in the next two sections.

ADABAS

A utility may be used to obtain a database status report which provides the following information:

— External storage allocations for the Associator and Data Storage.

— Free space available in the Associator and Data Storage.

— Pending Checkpoint/Restart information.

— Complete Field Description for each file in the database.

— File coupling information.

The ADABAS logging facilities can optionally provide statistics for each session. This information, which is stored on a disk file, provides for each command:

— Name of program issuing the command;

— Time in, and Time out for the command;

— Number of buffers referenced;

— Number of physical accesses required;

— Response Code.

The utility report and the statistics can be used to manage and optimise the database. The information will allow inefficient programs to be detected. It also allows start up parameters, such as the maximum number of concurrent users in the multi-user mode, to be selected to give optimum performance. Any degradation can be detected and corrective action taken. For example, a volatile file may need reorganising.

DMS 1100

The physical design of the database can have a significant effect on performance. Physical design includes the choice of location modes and record placement strategies. The page sizes selected for each area and the buffer pool size can also influence performance.

At system generation time DMS 1100 can be tailored to support selected facilities. The code supporting facilities like Index Sequential processing, pointer arrays, etc, can optionally be omitted from DMS 1100 in order to reduce its size.

DMS 1100 can optionally make execution statistics available to run-units. These statistics can be used for monitoring performance. A utility provides a status report on the physical state of the database areas.

IDMS

The performance of database programs is influenced by the choice of location modes and the record placement strategies. The page size and the number of buffers also need to be selected for optimum performance.

IDMS collects statistics for each run-unit which include:

— number of Pages read;

— number of Pages written;

— number of Page references;

— number of DML calls.

A run-unit may access its own statistics (ACCEPT verb) or a user written procedure may be used to collect this information. An examination of these statistics allows run-units which are running inefficiently to be identified. For example, an excessive number of page reads could mean that insufficient buffers have been allocated or a large set is being read repeatedly.

A utility is provided which reports on the physical state of the database areas. It reports the amount and distribution of free space, the number of occurrences of each record type in an area and information about their distribution.

Some ICL implementations allow part of the database to be loaded into virtual storage. Specified ranges of pages are read into special buffers, in virtual storage, which are not reused. This feature can improve the performance of parts of the database that are very heavily used for retrieval.

IMS-DL/1

The performance of the DL/1 system can be influenced in a number of ways. The database design and choice of DL/1 access method can affect access performance. Physical file attributes (such as control interval or block size) and buffering strategies can be altered in order to tune the system.

DL/1 generates performance monitoring statistics which may be used to monitor the system. These statistics can be used to determine whether a tuning exercise has achieved its objectives. A VSAM report can be used to monitor the use of file space.

TOTAL

Performance can be influenced through the physical definition and loading of the TOTAL files. The blocksizes, number of buffers and buffer pooling requirements can be selected and adjusted for optimum performance. Master Data Sets should have enough free space to minimise the number and length of synonym chains. The system does, however, automatically optimise synonym chains by removing or reducing their length when a deletion makes this possible. Variable Entry Data Sets should be loaded by their prime linkpath so that related records are physically close to each other.

TOTAL can optionally produce run time statistics which may be used to monitor the performance of the system. A utility is provided to report on the physical condition on the database files which reports the amount of free space in the files. Information about synonym chains and linkpaths is also available. These tools allow the state of the database to be monitored and degradation identified before it becomes serious.

STORAGE OPTIMISATION

This section describes the facilities offered by the five DBMSs for optimising the use of secondary storage. It discusses the possibility of holding the data in a compressed format in order to save disk space. The space management algorithm is also mentioned although a fuller discussion of this can be found in Chapter 5 under the heading of The Implementation of Data Structures. Any facilities which enable the placement of records on the database to be controlled are also described.

ADABAS

ADABAS stores data in a compressed format. Null fields (fields which have never been assigned a value) do not occupy any space in the physical record. Leading zeros on numbers and trailing blanks in character strings are also suppressed. These compression techniques are claimed to produce an average compression rate of 30% of the raw data requirement. An ADABAS database consisting of its Data Storage and its Associator may occupy less space than the raw data would occupy stored conventionally.

Space within an ADABAS file is never fragmented. When a record is deleted from a physical block the remaining data is relocated in order to make the free space contiguous at the end of the block. A load limit may be specified when the file is loaded in order to reserve space in each physical block for future additions. The space management mechanism can take additional data storage for the file if the existing data storage areas become full.

DMS 1100

DMS 1100 provides a number of mechanisms for controlling the way in which database storage is used. The location modes 'CALC', 'VIA', 'INDEX SEQUENTIAL' and 'DIRECT' determine how a record type is stored. A record type may be restricted to a specific subset, ie page ranges, of the AREA(s) in which it may be stored. It is also possible to force records of a given record type to be stored at least a specified minimum distance away from other records of the same type, which is particularly useful for owners of a VIA set.

The space management algorithm is designed to find free space with the minimum overhead. When a record is deleted it is flagged as deleted but it is not physically removed from the page containing it. The system will relocate the records up a page to physically delete the flagged records and make all the free space contiguous when it attempts to add a record and finds that there is insufficient space because of the fragmentation. A utility option is provided to perform this function, called compaction, offline.

The characteristics defined for an area allow some control over the management of storage. An area may be expanded dynamically by the system when necessary. Overflow pages may be specified, either pooled together at the end of an area or distributed throughout the area. A utility function allows the page size to be increased in order to make more space available. It is also possible to specify a load limit, which is effective on initial load, to reserve space within the pages of an area to cater for future updates.

Facilities within DMS 1100 allow data to be compressed if required. Database procedures may be used to compress/decompress a record or a field. The schema also provides facilities for replacing values which are either explicitly defined or contained in a table. This allows frequently occurring names, such as town names in an address, to be abbreviated.

IDMS

As with DMS 1100, IDMS allows the use of database storage to be controlled. The choice of location mode (CALC, VIA and DIRECT) influences the way in which records are stored. Record types may be limited to specified page ranges within an area. Records of a given type may also be forced to be stored a specified number of pages apart which is useful for ensuring that the owners of VIA sets have space around them for their members.

Space can also be reserved within the pages of an area to accommodate variable length records whose length increases as a result of modification. This reserved space cannot be used by records being added to the database.

Special space management pages distributed throughout each AREA document the availability of free space and enable the system to find free space efficiently. When a record is deleted the space occupied by it is usually available for reuse immediately. If a record participates in more than one set and prior linkages are not available, it is inefficient to delete the whole record immediately so it is logically deleted. Logically deleted records, which consist of just the pointer prefix, are deleted when the other linkages are traversed or they can be deleted explicitly by a utility. The free space within a page does not become fragmented. The records on a page are relocated when necessary to provide one contiguous block of free space.

A utility is available which increases the size of the pages within an AREA. This enables extra space to be provided quickly and easily.

The records on an IDMS database may be compressed in order to save storage space, or to encode the records for security reasons. Database procedures are used to accomplish this. Compression and decompression procedures are provided but these may be replaced by user written algorithms if required.

IMS-DL/1

When VSAM is used space freed by a deletion can be reused. If ISAM and OSAM are used, deleted records are only flagged as deleted; they are not physically removed until the files are reorganised.

As segments are deleted from a HDAM or HIDAM physical database (file) the free space within the VSAM ESDS is not optimised. The free space within a block is chained together. Remaining segments are not relocated, because physical pointers may address them, so free space may become fragmented.

When the physical DBD is generated a segment compression exit may be specified on each segment definition. The user is responsible for producing the compression routine.

TOTAL

When records are deleted from a Master or Variable Entry Data Set the space released is immediately available for reuse. The records stored in a TOTAL file have a fixed length so storage cannot become fragmented. TOTAL does not support any data compression facilities.

A load limit can be specified for each Variable Entry Data Set. This reserves space for records which are added to existing linkage paths within a cylinder of the file. New linkage paths are not started within the cylinder unless there is no cylinder below the load limit. This helps to group records within a linkpath together and may thus improve performance. (A cylinder is a physical subdivision of a file.)

ACCESS OPTIMISATION

This final section considers the facilities for optimising access provided by the five DBMSs. Access times should be considered while the database is being designed. Once the database has been implemented it is usually very difficult to significantly improve access performance without reorganising or restructuring the database.

ADABAS

ADABAS is well suited to random retrieval because its use of partially inverted file structures allows this to be done efficiently. If records are added to, or deleted from the database, or if descriptor fields are updated, ADABAS must update the Association Network to reflect the change. This involves changing the inverted lists in the index and possibly the address converter. The number and volatility of descriptor fields will therefore affect performance in an updating environment.

DMS 1100

Database access needs to be given careful consideration at the design stage when the location mode of the records is chosen. 'CALC' records will normally be accessible in one I/O operation if the page is not already in a memory buffer. If a page overflow condition has forced the required record onto an overflow page, the system may have to perform further I/O operations. Should there be a possibility of long calc chains forming then multiple calc chains may be specified in the schema to prevent this.

A location mode of 'VIA' allows an owner record to have its members clustered about it. An owner and its associated members will be stored on a page, or small group of pages. The entire set can therefore be accessed with a small number of I/O operations.

The 'DIRECT' location mode allows a record to be accessed in one I/O operation. The database key is used to access the record. This mode is normally avoided, except when speed is critically important.

Records stored with a mode of 'INDEX SEQUENTIAL' are stored in the physical order of their access keys, so sequential access will cause the database area to be read physically sequentially. If overflow has been permitted (ie overflow pages exist and NEXT/PRIOR pointers are defined for linking into the overflow pages) performance will degrade as records spill over into it.

The access efficiency of INDEXED records depends on the index structure. A number of accesses may be needed to search the index before the required record is read. An index is never updated so fragmentation never occurs. A Data Reorganisation Utility is used to maintain indexes when necessary.

The set linkages selected at the design stage also influence access optimisation. Deletions from a chained set without PRIOR pointers may force the system to read round the whole set to access the preceding record in order to reset its next pointer to bypass the record being deleted. If, while processing a set, it is necessary to access the owner and no OWNER pointers have been defined, the system will read round the set to find the owner. This is grossly inefficient if the set has a large number of members. The use of the POINTER ARRAY set mode may prove to be more efficient in this case.

IDMS

Access to the database needs to be considered at the design stage when the location mode of the records is decided. Records which have a location mode of 'CALC' can normally be accessed in an I/O operation unless of course the required Page is already in storage. If an overflow condition has forced the record onto another Page it is possible that a number of Pages may have to be read to locate the required record.

The 'VIA' location mode enables an owner record to have its member records clustered around it. The member records will therefore be stored together on a Page, or a small group of Pages if there are a large number of them. The owner and the entire set of members could be accessed with only a small number of I/O operations.

The 'DIRECT' location mode allows a record to be retrieved in one I/O operation because the direct key is the record's database key. This mode would normally be avoided except in situations where access speed is critically important.

The system accesses records directly when it is following a set since the pointers linking records are database keys. The set linkages chosen at the database design stage can also have a major effect on access optimisation. Deletions from a set without PRIOR pointers may force the system to read round the set in order to adjust the NEXT pointer of the preceding record to bypass the record being deleted. If a programmer frequently needs to access the owner of a member, and if the set does not have OWNER pointers, the system will have to read round the set until it finds the owner which could be grossly inefficient if the set is large.

IMS-DL/1

The choice of DL/1 access method for a physical database (file) can have a major impact on performance and needs to be considered at the design stage. In general when non-sequential processing is required HDAM should be used. HDAM provides direct access to the root segment with a minimum number of I/O requests. However HDAM does not allow sequential processing in root key order unless the physical sequence is arranged to correspond to the logical sequence by the user supplied randomising algorithm.

If HDAM is unsuitable HIDAM should be used instead. Access to a HIDAM physical database (file) involves an index search which causes additional I/O operations. When secondary indexes are used DL/1 must maintain them so the index maintenance processing overhead has to be considered.

When new segments are inserted in HDAM or HIDAM physical databases (files), DL/1 attempts to place them within a specified distance of related segments in order to optimise access. If no space is available the segments are inserted near the end of the file.

Physical database record types should be designed carefully. Performance will be improved if the most frequently accessed segment types are placed on the left and at the highest possible level of the data structure; these segments may then be stored in the same physical block. Segment sizes and twin chain lengths may also affect performance.

A feature called the Multiple Data Set Option may be used to optimise access (IMS only). A data structure may be split into two at the root level. Each part of the structure may then be stored in a separate file. Consequently two access paths may be optimised.

TOTAL

The use of a control field as a hashing key to a Master Data Set results in the data normally being retrieved with one I/O operation. TOTAL optimises access to Master Data Sets by always minimising the length of synonym chains and by attempting to place synonym records as near to their preferred location as possible.

The use of pointers allows records in a Variable Entry Data Set to be retrieved with one I/O operation. TOTAL attempts to place records which are chained together by a linkpath as near to one another as possible in order to reduce the number of physical blocks of data that need to be read and reduce disk head seeking to a minimum. A record may of course be linked into a number of different linkpaths. Only one of these can be optimised, usually the most frequently used path, called the Primary Linkpath.

Once a record has been stored in a Variable Entry Data Set it will *not* be relocated by the system in an attempt to organise the data more efficiently. Such a record will be addressed by one or more Master Data Sets and other Variable Entry records will address it through their linkage field.

Appendix 1

Bibliography

1   *Evaluation and Implementation of Database Systems: Database Software Descriptions, Part 2: Mainframe Systems*, NCC Publications, 1980.
    (The major part of this book is based on the material contributed to this report by the author. It is one of twelve reports resulting from a European database study in which the NCC (UK), GMD (Germany), INRIA (France) and CNR (Italy) collaborated.)

2   B Davis, *The Selection of Database Software*, NCC Publications, 1977.

3   B Davis, *Database in Perspective*, NCC Publications, 1980.

4   J Martin, *Computer Database Organisation*, Prentice-Hall. 1977.

5   C J Date, *An Introduction to Database Systems*, Addison-Wesley, 1977.

    Computer-Based Information Systems, M352, Open University Press, 1980

    There are three 'Blocks', ie three publications:

6   BLOCK I: A) Informations Systems   B) Why Database?

7   BLOCK II: A) Conceptual Modelling   B) Logical Modelling.

8   BLOCK III: Database Software

    (Note: These three publications should be read in conjunction with J Martin, *Principles of Database Management*. There are also other components to the course such as 'Activity' booklets.)

9   J Martin, *Managing the Database Environment*, Volume I, Savant
    Institute, 1980.

Specific DBMS Documentation: Consult the appropriate vendors for
up-to-date information about their products and available documentation.

Appendix 2

Glossary of Acronyms

ADABAS	Adaptable DAta BAse System. The name of the database management system marketed by Adabas Software Limited.
ADAM	Adabas Direct Access Method (ADABAS).
ADAMINT	ADAbas Macro INTerface (ADABAS).
CODASYL	COnference of DAta SYstems Languages.
CICS	Customer Information Control System. Software which supports on-line transaction processing. It is marketed by IBM. CICS/VS runs under the operating systems which support Virtual Storage.
DBA	Data Base Administrator or Data Base Administration.
DBD	Data Base Description (DL/1).
DBDL	Data Base Definition Language (TOTAL).
DBMOD	Data Base MODule (TOTAL).
DBMS	Database Management System.
DDL	Data Description Language.
DL/1	Data Language One. The name of a database management system marketed by IBM. DL/1 is the database manager used by IMS.
DMCB	Device Media Control Block (IDMS).

DMCL   Device Media Control Language (IDMS
                            -Cullinane product).

DML   Data Manipulation Language.

DMR   Data Management Routine (DMS 1100).
                            The nucleus or run-time component of DMS 1100.

DMS 1100   Data Management System 1100.

DOS   Disc Operating System.
                            An IBM produced operating system which runs on
                            small and medium sized 370 and 4300 range
                            machines. DOS/VS and DOS/VSE support Vir-
                            tual Storage.

ENVIRON/1   The name of the teleprocessing software marketed
                            by Cincom Systems Limited.

IBM   International Business Machines Limited.

ICL   International Computers Limited.

IDMS   Integrated Data Management System. The name
                            of the database management system marketed by
                            Cullinane and ICL.

IMS   Information Management System.
                            IMS comprises two major components:
                            IMS/DC – the Data Communication or telepro-
                            cessing software and IMS/DB – the Data Base
                            management software which is in fact DL/1.

ISN   Internal Sequence Number (ADABAS).

I/O   Input/Output.

MVS   Multiple Virtual Storage.
                            The name of an operating system that runs on large
                            IBM mainframes.

OS 1100   Operating System 1100. The name of the operat-
                            ing system which runs on the Sperry Univac 1100
                            series machines.

PCB   Program Communication Block (IMS-DL/1).

PSB   Program Specification Block (IMS-DL/1).

RPG   Report Program Generator.
                      A high-level programming language.

SDDL   Subschema Data Definition Language (DMS 1100).
                      Subschema Data Description Language (IDMS).

SDL   Service Description Language (IDMS-ICL).

TOTAL   The name of Cincom Systems Limited database management system.

TPS 1100   Transaction Processing System 1100.
                      A teleprocessing system which runs on Sperry Univac's 1100 series machines.

VME   Virtual Machine Environment.
                      The name of one of the operating systems which runs on ICL's 2900 series of machines.

VSAM   Virtual Storage Access Method.
                      An access method supported by IBM operating systems which support Virtual Storage.

Appendix 3

Index

Names and numbers in italics refer to complete sections of text.